A PHOTOGRAPHIC GUIDE TO

SE   S

OF

NEW ZEALAND

WADE DOAK

NEW
HOLLAND

First published in 2003 by New Holland Publishers (NZ) Ltd
Auckland • Sydney • London • Cape Town

218 Lake Road, Northcote, Auckland 0627, New Zealand
Unit 1, 66 Gibbes Street, Chatswood, NSW 2067, Australia
86-88 Edgware Road, London W2 2EA, United Kingdom
80 McKenzie Street, Cape Town 8001, South Africa

www.newhollandpublishers.co.nz

Publishing manager: Matt Turner
Design and typesetting: Julie McDermid
Editor: Brian O'Flaherty

Doak, Wade.
A photographic guide to sea fishes of New Zealand / Wade Doak.
Includes bibliographical references and index.
ISBN 978 1 877246 95 1
1. Marine fishes–New Zealand–Identification. 2. Marine fishes–
New Zealand–Pictorial works. I. Title.
597.1770993-dc 21

Colour reproduction by Pica Digital Pte Ltd, Singapore
Printed by Times Offset (M) Sdn Bhd, Malaysia

10 9 8 7 6 5 4

Front cover photograph: snapper (*Pagrus auratus*).
Back cover photograph: splendid perch, male (*Callanthias australis*).
Spine photograph: porcupinefish (*Allomycterus jaculiferus*).
Title page photograph: crimson cleanerfish (*Suezichthys aylingi*).

Contents

Foreword *by Dr Tony Ayling*

It is common practice to regard fishes as dumb objects whose lives are controlled purely by blind instinct. We relegate fishes to the same level as we do most of the lowest animals: unthinking, unfeeling and not conscious of the world around them, acting and reacting at the bid of instinctive cues. This attitude is not confined to the person in the street who understandably sees fish only as slabs of flesh to be bought, or an unseen prey to be lured onto a fishhook and hauled struggling to the fry pan. It is shared by those who are more closely associated with the sea and fishes, such as divers and fishermen and also, unfortunately, by academic researchers. Ichthyologists (fish scientists) and ethologists (behavioural scientists) in their studies of fishes and fish behaviour have neglected to consider fishes as other than items to be categorised and behaviour patterns to be put into interconnected boxes: 'action', 'triggering response', 'reaction'.

As a field marine biologist studying the ecology of encrusting communities as well as fish behaviour I have spent a lot of time under water watching and being watched by fishes. Close contact with reef fishes has slowly brought a realisation of the inaccuracies of the widespread, unthinking attitude towards them. To help readers consider Wade Doak's book with a more understanding attitude and help them to put into the right context the innumerable observations and notes on reef fish ecology and behaviour that it contains, I shall try to dispel some common misconceptions by presenting ideas and observations that have helped to change my own view of fishes. In doing so, I hope to build up a picture of a fish's perception of the world he lives in and show how this influences his day-to-day activities. To make this task easier and at the risk of being criticised for anthropomorphic thinking, I will refer to fishes as individuals by the common masculine pronoun 'he'. I am not being anthropomorphic but rather stacking things slightly in the fish's favour.

An important premise that must be stressed before I start, however, is the importance of viewing the lives of fishes against the background of the evolutionary theory of natural selection. Every aspect of their behaviour and ecology must be interpreted on the basis of the advantage given to an individual fish; how does it increase his chances of survival and, more importantly, how does it increase his chances of contributing successfully to the next generation? With this in mind, let us turn to the fishes and their lives.

Any diver who frequently returns to a favourite diving location will probably have noticed that some distinctive fish individuals are in the same place time after time, sometimes over a period of many years. This is because most reef fish are territorial or home ranging and spend their entire life in a limited area. The size of a fish's home range naturally depends on his size and behaviour. A small blenny may never venture out of an area the size of a small room, whereas a large red moki probably ranges over many thousands of square metres of sea bottom.

This being the case, it is clearly an advantage for a fish to learn and remember all the bottom features within his home range and the position of each of these. Using this terrain memory a fish knows exactly where he is at any time and can instantly take the best escape route to safety should danger threaten. Besides this, each fish knows the best feeding places within his home range, the best spots to rest and survey the surroundings. He also has a secure refuge where he can rest at night. All these factors combine to reduce the stresses of each fish's life and increase his chances of survival.

A young fish knows only a very small patch of bottom terrain but as he grows and wanders over a larger and larger area so does the size of his known range increase. Within this limited world the fish is secure and his behaviour reflects this security. But if for some reason he is forced into an area outside his knowledge he will begin to behave nervously, getting more and more agitated until some watchful predator finds him an easy, if somewhat confused, meal. This was vividly demonstrated when I observed the release of a captured male Sandager's wrasse in a strange area a kilometre from his home territory. He was immediately attacked and driven off, not only by other males of his own kind but also by many other normally peaceful reef fish, some many times smaller than him.

This brings us to another aspect of a fish's view of the world, one that seems self-evident after it is pointed out. Each fish must be able to recognise instantly all the different species he is likely to meet during his day-to-day activities. He must learn from a very early age not to confuse the harmless goatfish lying on the bottom with the dangerous, predatory scorpionfish. A John dory must know that he cannot eat an indigestible leatherjacket and has to decide immediately what species he is looking at or he may miss out on a meal. Even in situations that are not a matter of life or death, empty belly or full, it is still an advantage to be able to recognise each species and know details of its behaviour and habits.

More importantly, as most marine fish have a long planktonic larval stage and offspring usually end up in an area far from their parents and often inhabited by markedly different fish fauna, this information cannot be inherited. An extreme example of this is the many species of fishes that arrive as larvae from Australia in the Tasmania current and settle around Northland's offshore islands. The index of fish species must, then, be learned by a young fish, and learned quickly and correctly if he is to survive. Rather than inheriting a set of instinctive reactions to the different fishes he is likely to meet, a young fish inherits a good memory and the sense to keep clear of all other fishes until he has learned the features and habits of each species. It is apparent from all this that most fishes are very visual animals, relying on sight for most of their activities. When the water is dirty these fishes cease normal activities and shelter on the bottom until the return of clearer conditions.

The ideas and concepts of a fish's view of the world presented here, if kept in mind by readers as they use this book, will bring a deeper understanding and appreciation of fishes. For the ichthyologist and ecologist it provides an avenue that may bring new insights and discoveries. For my part this approach has brought an awareness that makes diving and fish watching far more personally satisfying.

Introduction: a community of reef fishes

This book describes many bony or teleostean reef fishes of New Zealand belonging to the Super Class PISCES, Class OSTEICHTHYES. The text discusses their habits by day and night, their modes of life, diet and relation to their surroundings. It does not include the cartilaginous fishes (the sharks and rays) belonging to the Class CHONDRICHTHYES, a full treatment of which would lie beyond the book's scope.

First, the text considers the more primitive bony fishes: eels, lizardfish, cods, John dory, golden snapper and scorpionfishes. But the greatest diversity of all is among the perch-like fishes (Order Perciformes), where the body plan has offered the greatest scope for adaptation. Most typical and generalised of the whole order are the serranids or groupers which are, like many primitive fishes, basically bottom-dwelling, fish-eating carnivores. Within this order we see diversification from these to high-speed pelagic carnivores: the carangids such as the kingfish; to coastal grazers such as the latridae (red moki, porae and tarakihi) and our biggest single family, the labrids or wrasses; to the most advanced and specialised in form: the tetraodontids, which include triggerfishes, pufferfishes and sunfishes.

That the pink maomao (in the family Serranidae) so closely resembles the quite unrelated blue maomao (of the family Scorpidae) is an excellent example of parallel evolution or convergence by which animals occupying similar niches develop outward resemblances in their fin and swimming patterns, and in their mouths and dentition.

This convergence may lead us into the error of trying to identify fishes according to outward resemblances, and so we are surprised to learn that the pink maomao is closely related to the grouper and quite remote from the blue maomao. With both maomao the shared habit of plankton feeding has led to such a similarity of form that the popular names suggest a relationship. To identify and fully understand our reef fishes their true relationships should be appreciated.

The fishes of New Zealand are part of the Indo-Pacific fish fauna, by far the richest in the world. Extending more than halfway around the globe, from East Africa to the Hawaiian and Polynesian islands, the Indo-Pacific region contains representatives of almost all the known families of marine fishes. Its many islands and continents provide a great diversity of habitats and it is probable that from this great basin most of the fishes of the world were distributed. As new species developed, they extended their ranges, giving rise to populations that split again and again.

The Contents page lists in taxonomic order all the families represented in this text with the common names of member species. From this the relationships between species can be understood.

Of the fishes described in this book around two-thirds are shared with south-east Australia, Queensland or subtropical islands to the north of New Zealand. Many New Zealand fishes probably originated from these areas and new species are still arriving.

The distribution range of each fish is described in the text. However, distribution maps have been omitted because they can be confusing and misleading: there are large gaps in current knowledge of fish distribution (especially of fishes on the west coast); different species may inhabit areas sporadically or vary in their range considerably; climate change or over-exploitation can alter distribution too.

Some species have been observed over a long period of time; comparatively little is known of some species. The species accounts differ accordingly.

Each individual description is headed with the species' common and scientific names plus the total length (TL) of the fish in centimetres.

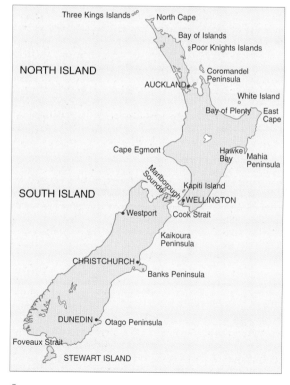

Fish design

The earliest known ancestors of the bony or teleostean fish were covered with heavy armour plate. Lacking swim bladders, their negatively buoyant bodies had to maintain constant movement to provide lift, otherwise they would fall to the bottom. This forward movement limited their modes of feeding and hence their range of success: such fishes would not be able to hover and feed in the water currents or graze the rock surfaces.

A parallel lineage, the cartilaginous fishes consisting of sharks and rays, has been rather limited by the lack of a swim bladder. Consequently, these are mostly large, roving carnivores, rather stereotyped in their habits, either living on the bottom, like rays and dogfishes, or swimming about freely, like sharks.

The most successful design was the bony fish. Supported by a swim bladder, and no longer needing to use muscular energy to hover or hold their position, these fishes could develop many novel shapes and forms. Teleost fish range from 3.6 m to 12 mm. Most are at the lower end of this range. Since more food niches are open to small animals there has been a proliferation of fish species, which now number around 20,000.

The teleost is basically a mobile pair of jaws propelled by segmented muscles and a set of pliant fins. It is streamlined for minimal water resistance and the body muscles are supported by a flexible backbone. Through a set of 'gill pumps' oxygen is obtained to release energy from foodstuffs. As teleosts are cold-blooded animals, no energy is needed to maintain body heat. An elaborate brain lies at the end of the spinal cord, protected by a bony skull. Nerve fibres supply the spinal cord and brain with external information from a complex range of sense organs: eyes, internal ears, nasal organs and taste buds on the head, and the tactile nerves and the unique lateral line system along the body. Depending on the fish's mode of feeding and respiration, its head takes a wide variety of shapes and forms: from the prey-engulfing maw of the groper, to the delicate tube-mouth of the Lord Howe Island coralfish, and the slender, sharp-toothed jaws of the grey moray.

The development of efficient respiration enabled the streamlined fish to cleave through its element with much more vigour than most other marine animals. The air we breathe contains 20 per cent oxygen, but in sea water there is only 1.8 per cent dissolved oxygen for the fishes to extract. While forward movement increases the intake of water for fast-moving pelagic fishes, sedentary fishes need huge heads and large gill covers or opercula to pump an adequate supply.

Lifestyle also determines the shape and development of the fins. Basically the fish has two sets of paired fins that correspond to our own arms and legs: the pectoral fins and the pelvic fins (sometimes called ventral fins). Along the back are the dorsal fins, from one to three in number. Beneath is the anal fin and at the rear the tail or caudal fin.

When swimming a fish does not simply wag its tail. In fact,

three different styles of propulsion (observation sometimes helpful for species identification) have been distinguished:

- **Anguilliform swimming:** contractions of the body muscles produce side-to-side undulations passing down the full length of the body, increased in efficiency by a laterally compressed tail (eels, cods, some triplefins and some blennies).
- **Carangiform swimming:** since the front part of the fish has lost flexibility, undulations are confined almost entirely to the rear half or third of the body length (pelagic fishes and many reef fishes).
- **Pectoral swimming:** a specialised form of propulsion involving small rowing movements of the pectoral fins (wrasses, coralfish, blue cod).

The fish's pectoral fins provide lift and, aided by the swim bladder, enable it to hover. They also serve as brakes and for pivotal turns, especially among plankton feeders. The pelvic fins may be in front of or behind the pectoral fins or, in some cases, non-existent. These fins provide equilibrium and prevent pitching. They are used as an undercarriage for bottom-resting species.

The deep-bodied leatherjacket and porcupinefish have pectoral fins high on their sides but no pelvic fins. Moray eels, with their undulatory swimming, have dispensed with both pelvic and pectoral fins. The dorsal and anal fins are stabilisers: they prevent rolling and aid the fish when turning. The dorsal fin also serves to maximise the body area in aggressive and sexual displays. Both these fins and the caudal fin may bear species-typical markings for those purposes.

The caudal fin varies widely in shape and function. With the eel it is just a continuation of the dorsal and anal fins. With high-speed pelagic fishes its lunate design minimises friction drag.

For the wrasses the caudal fin serves mainly as a rudder except for flight reactions, while propulsion comes from a sculling action of the pectorals. To the bizarre sunfish the caudal fin is just a vertical steering flap, with little propulsive function. The main propulsion is from sculling by the tall dorsal and anal fins.

Within the dense hydrosphere, the fish has sensory experience quite different from our own. Since water is incompressible, energy disturbances in the form of vibrations are transmitted with great fidelity to a variety of sensory nerve endings or receptors on the lateral line and the head.

Under water, sound waves travel four and a half times faster than in air. The fish has no eardrums: its whole body, especially the swim bladder, acts as a sound receptor. The internal ear receives the sound stimuli and also acts as a balance organ.

Although the dispersion of chemicals in water is slower than in air, chemoreception, combining taste and smell, is a highly developed sense in a world where vision is often limited. Most fish have nostrils on either side of the snout, unconnected with the respiratory system. Each nostril consists of an inlet pore and an outlet. Those of the moray eel are most apparent: a pair of mobile ciliated tubes that increase chemical sensitivity.

Fishes also have taste buds on many parts of their bodies; some have them on sensory barbels and even over their skin. We taste substances dissolved in our saliva. Fishes live in water, an excellent solvent to convey substances to their taste organs. Also distributed over the skin are myriads of fine nerve endings sensitive to touch and to changes in temperature, salinity and pressure.

Unique to fishes and some amphibians is a 'distance-touch' sense provided by the organs of the lateral line. Along each side of the body are mucus-filled canals. This system may also extend in three rows of pores over the head, especially obvious in the moray. Hairlike sense organs project into this fluid and vibrations received by these initiate impulses to the central nervous system. The fish can thus sense any local disturbance of the field and from the bounce back of vibrations from its own movements can even detect its proximity to surrounding objects. With this radar system the fish can 'feel' where it is located and what is moving in the vicinity.

Light penetration varies greatly in the sea according to depth and clarity, but for the reef fishes in this book vision is very important. The lens of a fish's eye bulges beyond the surface of the head. This is necessary for all-round vision as the fish lacks a neck. Such an eye, it has recently been discovered, provides long-sighted vision laterally but the clearest images in the forward field. The fish has thus the most effective vision where most needed: when seeking food, stalking prey or avoiding enemies. Its retinal mechanisms are well adapted to life in the sea, being especially developed to increase contrast in poor conditions, and to register the slightest movements. Those fish that rely on sight for capturing food, locating their refuge or perceiving mating signals have the finest vision. Reef fishes have colour vision very much like our own. Some can distinguish 24 different spectral hues and may even exceed our spectral range at the violet end, with very good discrimination of varied shades of grey.

Many sight-feeding species have binocular vision. Owing to the position of their eyes, or their protruding sockets, both eyes can be focused on prey, enabling precise perception of distance. This may be seen in the predatory scorpionfish, the John dory, the flounder and many plankton feeders.

Some nocturnal fishes rely on vision to detect planktonic prey. Their relatively large eyes are especially adapted to collecting all possible light and divers have seen them selectively feeding on moonlit nights.

Colour has three important functions in fishes. It is used to conceal, to disguise or to advertise. The most common form of camouflage is cryptic coloration, by which the fish resembles the shades and hues of its surroundings: fish over light bottoms are light coloured, those in weeds and shaded areas are dark. Some species have the ability to change colour to match the background perfectly.

By means of an optical principle called obliterative counter shading, many fish reduce their visibility to predators or prey.

Dorsal surfaces, normally directed towards the light, are counter-shaded by darkening whereas the abdomen, usually in shadow, is lightened. These tones, properly graded, make the fish appear optically flat, like a shadow. The kingfish is an excellent example and can be contrasted with the cave-dwelling slender roughy in which the effect is reversed. In many cases (red moki, pufferfish) the effect is also used with other forms of concealment.

By disruptive coloration the outline of the fish is broken down into irregular patches of contrasting colour. These draw attention away from the fish's total shape. Vertical stripes, oblique bands and large dots all serve this purpose. Often these are used to conceal vital areas of the body: fins are black, eyes are masked; the tail bears an eyespot or ocellus (as with the juvenile black angelfish), making it seem more like the head.

Colour is used for advertisement by many species, notably the Lord Howe coralfish and the wrasses.

Classification

For classification I have used the most widely accepted system, that of Greenwood, Rosen, Weitzman and Myers: 'Phyletic Studies of Teleostean Fishes, with a Provisional Classification of Living Forms' (*Bulletin of the American Museum of Natural History*, Vol. 131, Article 4, New York, 1966). Their words aptly summarise my own thoughts on fishes: 'Their diversity is astounding. Estimates of the number of living species vary from somewhat under 20,000 up to 40,000. The facts that discovery of new species and genera is still commonplace, and that new forms of considerable evolutionary importance (and many recently described deep sea forms) are still being discovered at a surprising rate, demonstrate that we are further from a reasonably complete knowledge of living teleosts than we are of any other large, non-piscine vertebrate group.'

The Contents page lists the families represented in this text. Family names also appear in the coloured tabs in the margins of each page. Variations in conventional order within some families are due to the demands of layout this format imposes.

Although common names are highlighted in the fish descriptions for ease of reference, all fishes are listed by their scientific names so that their affinities with related species may be easily seen. The scientific names are those in current use although, due to ongoing research and discovery, some may be superseded within a short space of time. The common names given are those that are generally recognised. Both common names and scientific names are listed in indexes.

For the scientific names of the species in this text I am primarily indebted to Dr Malcolm Francis of the National Institute of Water and Atmospheric Research Limited: one of the most authoritative workers on New Zealand fishes and author of several books about their identification.

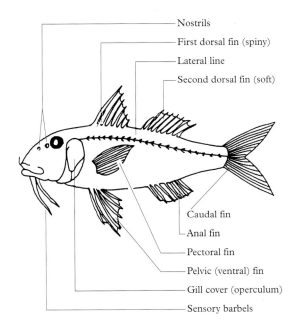

- Nostrils
- First dorsal fin (spiny)
- Lateral line
- Second dorsal fin (soft)
- Caudal fin
- Anal fin
- Pectoral fin
- Pelvic (ventral) fin
- Gill cover (operculum)
- Sensory barbels

Anatomy of a fish (example is a goatfish).

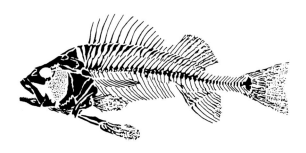

The skeleton of a fish resembles an arrow designed to guide and propel a set of jaws.
(N.B. Marshall, *The Life of Fishes*. Weidenfeld and Nicholson, London, 1965.)

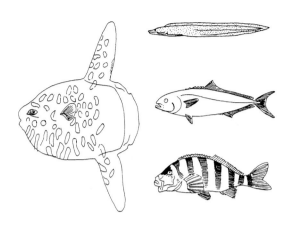

From the perfect spindle form (kingfish, centre right), fishes have adapted their bodies in many extremes to suit lifestyle: from the circular sunfish to the elongate eel and deep-bodied red moki (bottom right).

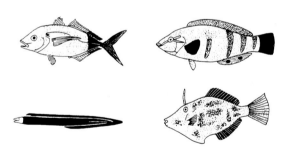

While many fishes such as the trevally (top left) are propelled by the tail and tail fin, some like the spotty (top right) use a sculling action of the pectorals. With eels power comes from travelling waves of curvature along their entire length. Stiff-bodied leatherjackets just ripple dorsal and anal fins.

(Sue Thompson, *Fish of the Marine Reserve.* Leigh Laboratory, 1981.)

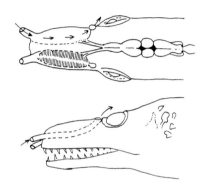

Fishes with fast start tails achieve rapid acceleration from rest by a process of bending and twisting.
(Heinrich Hertel, *Structure, Form and Movement*. Reinhold, New York, 1966.)

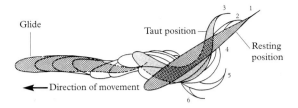

The nasal organs of eels are 100 times more efficient than those of humans. As with most fishes, water is drawn through the front nostril, over a set of odour receptors, to exit by the rear aperture.
(N.B. Marshall, *The Life of Fishes*. Weidenfeld and Nicholson, London, 1965.)

Some fishes have the chameleon ability to change colour rapidly. At the centre, colour cells with black pigment are expanded. Surrounding cells are contracted to a dot.
(N.B. Marshall, *The Life of Fishes*. Weidenfeld and Nicholson, London, 1965.)

Eels

There are five New Zealand moray eels: the mosaic, grey, speckled, yellow and mottled. Other eels described on the following pages are the conger eel and snake eel.

Eels are adapted to living in narrow crevices and holes, where they find both food and shelter. With such a habitat, many features of the normal fish anatomy were unnecessary or even a disadvantage. The eel's body has become long and slender, to enable it to insinuate itself into confined areas. This involves an exaggerated swimming action throwing the whole body into a series of elegant transverse waves, which increase in amplitude as they pass back along the body. There is also a reduction of tail fin, abandonment of pelvic fins and the development of one continuous dorsal/anal fin. While river eels and congers still have pectoral fins, the morays have lost these too.

For a fish to withdraw backwards into narrow fissures, bony gill covers would be an encumbrance. The eel has an arrow-like skull and its gill openings are reduced to small slits behind the pectoral fins or, with the morays, just a hole on either side of the head. By having such tiny gills the eels are exceptions to the rule for bottom dwelling fishes, which generally have large-capacity gill chambers working as suction pumps, to ensure adequate ventilation while resting inert for long periods. Lacking these large gill covers, to produce a bellows action the eel must keep its mouth open almost continuously.

The eyes of eels differ from those of other fishes. They are covered with a protective skin; in addition, the iris is able to contract, thus controlling the amount of light reaching the retina. Most fish are unable to do this and are dazzled when we shine bright lights on them at night.

As the moray breathes, water is forced towards the gills by a swallowing action. Flow of water back out of the mouth is prevented by means of small, muscular ring-valves or sphincters at the internal gill slits. This explains the malevolent appearance of the gaping jaws.

For tracking their prey at night or in dark regions, eels have a highly developed sense of smell. The nostrils are spread well apart on the snout to provide accurate direction-finding as the head veers from side to side sampling the water currents. These nasal apertures are tubular, lined with tiny hair-like cilia which beat inwards to draw water into two large nasal cavities. As water flows over the olfactory organs, receptor organs in the delicately folded skin are able to sense the smallest odour traces. The water passes out through the rear part of the nostrils just in front of and slightly above the eye.

For backward movement and sinuous swimming, scales would be a hindrance. River eels have only very tiny scales beneath a thick coating of mucus; congers and morays have no scales at all.

Mosaic moray *Enchelychore ramosa* TL 180 cm

At times the mosaic moray looks ghostly white. It is a strange sight, with its slender, curving jaws swaying beneath a rocky ledge. On other occasions the olive-green mosaic pattern is predominant and the moray is much better concealed. The jaws of this moray cannot close fully even when it snaps its mouth shut. The canine teeth are extremely fine, long, translucent and needle sharp. Such jaws could inflict very painful wounds, yet the mosaic moray will let a diver approach within centimetres without the least sign of attack. Initially it just freezes and glowers, then it begins to withdraw, backing off very slowly at first, then with increasing rapidity, always keeping its eyes fixed on the diver. A body's length away, it turns and flees. If followed, it will stop, draw into a rocky recess and repeat the performance. Most fishes would continue to flee and could easily evade a diver, but the mosaic moray prefers to face danger, perhaps because its fierce mien should be sufficient to discourage any aggressor. The mosaic moray can be found from northern New Zealand to East Cape. It feeds on crabs, shrimps and small fishes.

Grey moray *Gymnothorax nubilus* TL 100 cm

The grey moray is the most slender and the smallest of the five New Zealand morays. Its snout is longer and narrower than that of the yellow moray, more suited to probing into narrow fissures and cracks for its prey of crabs, shrimps and small fishes. Its nasal tubes are longer and the dorsal fin is very high and fleshy, with a light blue fringe. Although they are mostly seen in holes in the cliff, these morays frequently inhabit tube sponges or just entwine themselves among the fronds of kelp. One was observed living in the same sponge for many months. Sometimes they share their refuge with another of their species, or with a yellow moray, the twin heads rearing from a hole like a nest of vipers. At dusk all morays become active hunters, serpenting across the bottom, but the grey moray can often be seen stalking prey by day. For some strange reason the grey moray is occasionally seen right alongside the scorpionfish, or draped over its back – or even coiled on the back of a stingray! The grey moray is distributed from northern New Zealand to East Cape, and is found mostly around offshore islands.

Speckled moray *Gymnothorax obesus* TL 200 cm

Found in similar areas to the grey, the speckled moray, dark brown with fawn dots, has an especially powerful and massive head. Its speckled camouflage conceals it from its quarry and its teeth are very well designed for seizing prey, for which there is no possibility of release. Like those of all morays, the teeth yield to backward pressure, but snap into a locked position when pushed forward towards the mouth opening. If damaged or dislodged, new teeth grow to replace them. A pair of these undersea pythons was once observed locked in furious combat. This is the largest of our morays, and it feeds on crustaceans and small fishes. Its distribution ranges from northern New Zealand to East Cape.

Yellow moray *Gymnothorax prasinus* TL 150 cm

Although similar in diet and habits to the grey moray, yellow morays seem more aggressive and territorial. Two were watched fighting viciously for several minutes until both were ripped and torn in many parts of their bodies, and eventually the most heavily lacerated one fled along the cliff face. This may well have been a territorial squabble. Since crustaceans make up most of their diet, it is surprising to see yellow morays at night with ruby red shrimps swarming over their skin, possibly removing parasites. They also seek the services of coral shrimps, which clean their teeth. This is the most common of the moray eels, and ranges from northern New Zealand to Hawke Bay.

Mottled moray *Gymnothorax prionodon* TL 100 cm

Both the mottled and the mosaic morays have long, heavily armed jaws. They are far less abundant than the other three species, and seldom is there more than one individual in any one area. While the other species are attracted to a bait in wriggling confusion, these morays are not easily tempted to leave their holes. Large specimens, up to 1 m long, seem to prefer the greater depths. At times the brown ground colour of the skin can be so dark as to obscure the mottled pattern, but normally, where light levels are diminished, it is an effective camouflage. It must be remembered that flashlit photographs spoil this effect. Like the other morays, the mottled feeds on crustaceans and small fishes. It ranges from northern New Zealand to the Bay of Plenty.

Conger eel *Conger verreauxi* TL 200 cm

The conger eel is distinguished from the moray eel by its more normal, fish-shaped head, slightly flattened, and the presence of pectoral fins. Whereas the dorsal fin of the moray begins near the head, raising its profile, that of the conger begins much further back, above the tip of the pectoral fin. The gills are small slits and the eyes are oval and much bigger. The teeth are all fine, the outer row forming a cutting edge in each jaw; the upper jaw projects slightly beyond the lower jaw, suiting it better to bottom feeding. At night it leaves its lair to prey on crustaceans and small fishes. Once congers reach their maximum length the body just continues to thicken. As nocturnal predators of juvenile fishes, congers and morays would have an important role in regulating the populations of reef fishes. Since congers must live near the bottom, a buoyant swim bladder would be disadvantageous. In the eels the swim bladder retains its primitive condition and opens directly into the oesophagus; this explains why congers have been said to 'bark', releasing air from the swim bladder in explosive bursts. The conger eel occurs throughout New Zealand in rocky areas, although it is more abundant in the South Island.

OPHICHTHIDAE

W. Farrelly

The aptly named snake eel is the longest eel in our waters, averaging 1.3 m and reaching 2.5 m, but usually no more than 5 cm in diameter. With its flattened, rigid tail tip and thin, silvery grey body it is adapted to swimming rapidly through mud and sand and lurking with just jaws and eyes emergent, to ambush small prey, presumed to be crustaceans and small fishes. It has a pointed head, with a very large mouth extending to behind the eyes. For concealment its sharp teeth are translucent. It lives in sandy coastal waters and estuaries, and is sometimes seen in small colonies. Juveniles can sometimes be seen in shallow estuaries. This subtropical species is found in warmer waters around northern New Zealand.

Lizardfish *Synodus doaki* TL 25 cm

Lizardfishes have a single dorsal fin; the pelvic fins are sited on the abdomen, well back from the pectorals. In this position the pelvic fins serve the lizardfish as an undercarriage for resting on the bottom, steadied by the wing-like pectorals like a small fighter plane. Lizardfish are common on the Great Barrier Reef, but in New Zealand they were unknown until the spring of 1970, when they were discovered at the Poor Knights. At depths of 15–60 m they lurk in sandy areas and occasionally perch on rocky ledges or flat rocks adjacent to sand. Sometimes they may be buried to the snout in the sand. Springing off their pelvic fins, these fierce little predators (up to 25 cm long) can dart forward faster than the eye can follow, driven by their tails and planing down onto the sand with their pectorals. They are often seen in pairs, but I have seen one attack a larger lizardfish and drive it from its territory. Filtration of colour by the sea means the ruby-red of the lizardfish is transformed into a dark, nondescript pattern, merging the fish perfectly into its surroundings. A sporadic invader of our waters, it does not appear to spawn here. It is confined to northern New Zealand. The lizardfish is also known as the red lizardfish.

MORIDAE

Hovering by day beneath a deep overhang, the shy, bearded rock cod peers out at the diver. Its small, sinuous tail flexes and the pectorals beat gently, for it seldom rests on the bottom. In a flash it disappears into a dark fissure. At night, ranging over the rocky bottom and across the sand, these cods are everywhere, feeding on crabs, shrimps, octopus and small, sleepy fishes. The rock cod is a bottom-dwelling carnivore equipped with a large mouth and a single sensory barbel beneath its chin. Each jaw has an outer band of strong, conical teeth, followed by a narrow band of small, velvety ones. Its scales are small and its pelvic fins are in front of the pectorals, an unusual arrangement. Rock cod live in rock crevices and holes during the day. A pair has been seen in the same crevice for many years. Often solitary, they occasionally form groups of three or more. The rock cod is quite common and widespread throughout New Zealand around reefs and over rough ground.

Northern bastard cod *Pseudophycis breviuscula* TL 20 cm

Seldom seen by day but common in shallow, inshore areas by night swimming close to the bottom, this small, greyish pink, plumpish cod differs from the larger red cod, *Pseudophycis bachus* (total length 60 cm), by having a rounded tail fin, rather than square cut, and lacking the dark blotch on the head above the pectoral fin. The northern bastard cod ranges throughout New Zealand, especially over muddy seafloors. It takes seafloor invertebrates and small fishes.

Southern bastard cod *Pseudophycis barbata* TL 50 cm

This nocturnal predator of crabs and small fishes differs from the larger red cod, *Pseudophycis bachus*, in that its tail is more rounded and it lacks the black spot at the pectoral fin base. There are distinct black margins to the dorsal, anal and tail fins. The colour varies from red-brown to dark brown, paler beneath. Southern bastard cod is found throughout New Zealand, but mostly in the South Island, and especially over a muddy seafloor. Food consists of seafloor invertebrates and small fishes.

Orange clingfish *Diplocrepis puniceus* TL 10 cm

Life in the intertidal zone on open coast is very demanding for a fish. The orange clingfish has special adaptations for turbulence: its pelvic and pectoral fins are fused to form a suction disc so it can cling to boulders, while its flattened form reduces drag. Clingfishes vary in colour but females (larger) are generally red-pink above, yellow below. Males are olive or brown with darker markings. In winter they spawn and males guard the eggs of several females in nests beneath boulders. The eggs range in colour according to ripeness. The orange clingfish feeds on small shellfish and crustaceans. It is widespread throughout New Zealand, and restricted to this country.

Flying fish *Cypselurus lineatus* TL 45 cm

For plankton feeding just below the surface the flying fish has large eyes high on its head. For camouflage against the mirror of the surface its undersides are silver, and dark blue above. To escape predators in this vulnerable zone it has greatly enlarged pectoral fins. Swimming at high speed, the streamlined form breaks the surface, the enlarged lower tail lobe still beating rapidly until the widespread pectoral 'wings' give lift off. Now it glides some 50 m before splashing in or beating its tail for another flight. By night, flying fishes hover just below the surface. This is one of the rare opportunities for divers to see them: lights attract plankton and the flying fish may resume feeding, wings partly extended. Flying fishes occur in offshore surface waters around northern New Zealand.

Golden snapper *Centroberyx affinis* TL 55 cm

By day, dusky brown shadows hover in the twilight of an undersea cave. Swimming slowly in mid-water, seldom near the surface and never resting on the bottom, the golden snapper hide their burnished, shot-silk bodies in the gloom. In deep water they hover, barely moving, above a pinnacle. These are nocturnal feeders, awaiting the nightly invasion of the upper sea layers by swarms of animal plankton: copepods, krill and arrow worms, and small fishes, which feed on them. Triggered by the fall in light intensity, animal plankton rise each evening from the deeps to feed all night long on the rich plant plankton in the surface layers, dropping down again at sunrise. The golden snapper is part of this food chain and is normally found in deep water, right down to 200 m offshore, wherever plankton-carrying currents are richest. Sharp spines on the head, fins and gill plates, and the heavily armoured scales with serrated, razor-sharp edges, provide defence. The mouth has bands of minute teeth in both jaws. The jaws are protrusile, with an upward, gulping action for seizing prey that may be silhouetted against the starlight or lit by the pale blue fire of luminous plankton. Golden snapper can be found around northern New Zealand.

Slender roughy *Optivus elongatus* TL 12 cm

A close relative to the golden snapper, the slender roughy is a smaller fish that inhabits the deeper waters of the continental shelf and the abyssal waters below, but it also comes well within the range of skindivers. It occurs from northern waters south to Cook Strait, as well as at the Chatham Islands. By day it lurks beneath low rock ledges in the darkness. Occasionally, on overcast days or when light is poor because of turbidity, the slender roughy is seen in schools in the open like the golden snapper, but normally it seeks shelter all day, only emerging to feed at night, like its larger relative. For grabbing plankton by starlight its mouth opens almost vertically, well served by the large, forward-positioned eyes. Since the slender roughy shelters beneath ledges and in caves, most light reaching its body comes from below, bouncing off the cave floor. Accordingly, its underside is dark so that it reflects less light and its back is pale. This two-toned copper colouring, light above and dark below, is an example of reverse countershading, adapted to daytime concealment. Its tail has distinctive red-brown stripes on each lobe. In late summer tiny juveniles from summer spawnings swim in sheltered nooks.

ZEIDAE

A mid-water predator, cardboard thin, patterned with rapid-change camouflage, the John dory is barely visible head on. It is a master of illusion: a sea-going mouth with an eyespot on its side that distracts from the mouth. The high dorsal fin, with its extended rays, and the outspread tail are motionless in the water, stabilising the fish so perfectly that no movement or changing light patterns draw attention to its neutrally buoyant body. It is constantly oriented directly at the prey, which is composed mainly of fishes, with some mid-water crustaceans. All propulsion is provided by hardly perceptible undulations of the opposed anal and soft dorsal fins. Like a spectre it glides over the reef, often tilted obliquely to mimic a scrap of weed drifting on the current or, with the aid of the false eyespot, a fish. Its forward-mounted, protruding eyes provide true bifocal vision, essential for accurate estimation of distance. Within about 30 cm of the quarry, the jaws expand in a flash. The broad gill plates dilate, creating a fierce suction. Into a long tube the animal is gulped and the mouth snaps shut. Its small, prickly teeth are only for gripping. The John dory occupies a variety of habitats, mostly on the open sandy seafloor, and is widespread north of Cook Strait, but is rather uncommon further south.

SYNGNATHIDAE

W. Farrelly

It is difficult to grasp that the seahorse truly is a fish with its bony armour, horse-like head and long, segmented tail. So well is it camouflaged that the diver is lucky to see it at all. In sheltered inshore waters, harbours and estuaries, or among seaweed groves its colour is yellow and brown with darker spots, but this usually matches its habitat. Among colourful sponges and corals offshore it may be bright yellow or orange. The seahorse swims in a vertical stance, pectoral fins and dorsal rippling, tail trailing below as a stabiliser or coiling around stems, eyes swivelling as it stalks tiny crustaceans, either in mid-water or crawling over a frond. Like a vacuum cleaner the trumpet mouth slurps it in. Males have a kangaroo-style brood pouch in which the female lays her eggs for fertilisation and incubation. After about a month the pregnant male gives birth to minute replica seahorses. Pair bonds are permanent. In the summer spawning season males have multiple pregnancies. There are daily courtship dances with tail-linked promenades, twirlings and pirouettes while rival males engage in tail-wrestling jousts. The seahorse is widespread around New Zealand.

Smooth pipefish *Stigmatopora macropterygia* TL 40 cm

W. Farrelly

The pipefish is a streamlined version of the seahorse, matching it in almost every aspect. It has a slender snout, long dorsal fin and a slender, pointed tail, that has no fin. The smooth pipefish is golden-brown with twin rows of black spots. In contrast to the seahorse, it mostly inhabits seaweed groves, often where there is a swift tidal flow, mostly around the low-tide mark. It is restricted to New Zealand, and is found all around the coast, being especially widespread south of Cook Strait. Food consists of animal plankton, especially small crustaceans.

Spiny sea dragon *Solegnathus spinosissimus* TL 50 cm

W. Farrelly

W. Farrelly

Because the spiny sea dragon often lives beyond diver range it is more likely to be seen in Fiordland where special conditions bring the depths closer. Its lifestyle is very similar to the seahorse's except that this is a much larger fish, yellow-orange with yellow bands and spots and prickly armour, ranging over the sea cliff or clinging to a sea fan. Instead of a brood pouch there is a patch beneath the male's tail where the female lays her eggs. Food consists of small planktonic crustaceans. The spiny sea dragon occurs all around New Zealand, generally in the open ocean.

Scorpionfish *Scorpaena cardinalis* TL 60 cm

SCORPAENIDAE

Scorpionfish mainly eat fish: blennies, demoiselles and blue mao-mao have been found in them, along with crabs, shrimps and small octopus. They are nocturnal hunters ranging out over the bottom and up and down the cliff faces at night, when many fishes seek rest. Superbly camouflaged, their numerous dermal flaps and filaments closely resemble the encrusting sponges and bryozoans among which they lurk. The rags and tatters on the head and body may become pale green or white when they lie among kelp. Like many bottom fishes, the scorpionfish has no swim bladder for hovering; its greatly developed pectoral fins are used as props for resting. When it approaches prey, the scorpionfish makes a short, swift rush, propelled by these fan-like pectorals and the broad tail. The huge mouth yawns open to engulf the quarry with a combined sucking and grasping action. There is another reason for the large head. Inactive for long periods, like many bottom-lurkers it requires capacious gill chambers to irrigate its gills. With a gentle bellows action the outsized gill flaps can pump a steady flow across the gills without disturbing the immobile posture of the fish. Scorpionfish occur in northern New Zealand down to East Cape. It is also known as northern scorpionfish, red rock cod and grandfather hapuku.

33

SCORPAENIDAE

W. Farrelly

Extremely variable in coloration, from dull purplish brown to bright red, the dwarf scorpionfish is most distinguishable from its larger relative the scorpionfish (previous page) by the light-coloured saddle across its nape and gill covers. Unlike the scorpionfish, which ranges over the rocky seafloor and reefs, it may also be found in muddy estuaries at night. Food consists of seafloor invertebrates, including crustaceans, and occasionally small fishes. The dwarf scorpionfish is widespread around northern New Zealand. It is also known as red scorpionfish.

Sea perch *Helicolenus percoides* TL 45 cm

Cradled in a cup sponge, or nestling beneath a ledge, the sea perch is mainly a nocturnal hunter but will take a daytime meal whenever possible. In northern regions it is rarely seen in shallow waters. In cooler waters south of Kaikoura it reaches maximum size. As it penetrates northwards, the average size reduces to about 20 cm and it lives either in deep water beyond 60 m, or where there are moderate depths providing cool water inshore. The sea perch has larger eyes than the scorpionfish, set lower down on the head (suited to bottom feeding on crabs), whereas those of the scorpionfish protrude above the outline of the head (for attacking fish above), giving it a froglike snout and binocular vision. The body of the sea perch is more compressed laterally and its more splayed tail fin frequently can have an active propulsive role. The five red bands on its body are very distinct from the mottled camouflage of the scorpionfish. An active carnivore rather than a passive lurker, the sea perch is often seen in small groups of three or four, while the scorpionfish is solitary and would drive away intruders on its territory. The sea perch occurs throughout New Zealand waters, especially in the south. It is also called Jock Stewart.

Red gurnard *Chelidonichthys kumu* TL 40 cm

W. Farrelly

Although widespread around New Zealand, the red gurnard is not often within diver range. A light pink, orange-blotched bottom dweller, it feeds over sand or mud to depths of 150 m, digging for worms, shellfish or crabs with its bony snout. The enlarged, green, turquoise-rimmed, wing-like pectoral fins are lightly spotted, and have a dark blotch with white spots near the base. The fins have three special sensory rays for finding buried prey. These distinctive fins may also have a signalling function for courtship and aggression and enable it to walk over the bottom, often sideways, when feeding. Red gurnard is also known simply as gurnard.

An impressive sight, with its huge goggly eyes and great under-shot, pointed jaws, high jagged dorsal fin and powerful, square-edged tail, the hapuku is one of New Zealand's largest fishes and inhabits our entire continental shelf, aggregating around pinna-cles where prey fish school. Hapuku also eat soft-shell crayfish. At the Three Kings Islands in the late 1960s divers were once sur-rounded by a huge herd of hapuku, which came whirling up from the deeps like a maelstrom and played around them for 10 min-utes before vanishing into the dark blue. Unexploited populations like this are rare nowadays and have almost vanished from diver range. Much larger protection zones than existing marine reserves will be needed before their populations can recover. When popu-lations are not reduced by over-fishing, the hapuku is a gregarious animal and seldom swims alone. Herds used to be from 30 to 100 individuals of all sizes. Each year the hapuku herds would return from deeper waters to the same caves and clefts for their winter spawning season. The tragedy for the lost hapuku population lies in their biology: once hauled to the surface, their swim bladder expands irreversibly. Released undersize fish cannot descend and soon die. Hapuku is also known as groper. It was formerly placed in the family Percichthyidae (temperate basses).

Yellow-banded perch *Acanthistius cinctus* TL 60 cm

First discovered at the Poor Knights in January 1969, this rare grouper is another sporadic coloniser from subtropical waters and is unlikely to spawn here. Like its relatives, it is a lurking predator and spends the day within a small cave, probably ranging out at dawn and dusk to feed on small fishes and crustaceans. For a fish that lives in dimly lit waters, the pattern of markings on its body and head – six black bands on its body and two stripes radiating from the eye – is an excellent example of disruptive coloration. It is often seen in pairs near archways, usually below 20 m. Yellow-banded perch occurs on the east coast of Northland, mainly around offshore islands.

Gold-ribbon grouper *Aulacocephelus temmincki* TL 40 cm

R. Kempthorne

The gold-ribbon grouper was first reported at the Poor Knights in May 1968. Unlike the others, this small, slender grouper does not rest on the floor of a cave but hovers near the roof and beneath vaulting overhangs, usually at depths beyond 30 m. Its coloration is well suited to this habitat: the gold stripe on its back is a reversal of the usual obliterative countershading strategy used by most fishes, with the back much darker than the belly. Since this fish swims near the roof, most light reaching it comes from below, bouncing up from the entrance. Accordingly, its underside is dark, so as to reflect less light. The yellow stripe running through its eye has a disruptive effect, breaking the outline of the body and drawing attention away from its telescopic jaws. The gold-ribbon grouper is only marginal at the Poor Knights and probably originates from the Kermadec Islands. It can be found around offshore islands in Northland.

Spotted black grouper
Epinephelus daemelii TL 80 cm (200 cm in tropics)

In New Zealand waters spotted black grouper only reach about half their potential size but in tropical waters they grow to more than 2 m: massive, man-size bottom-dwellers. Whereas here they are small and solitary, there they form small groups of varying sizes. Individuals may live in the same cave for years. The lair usually has several alternative exits and the grouper hovers just off the bottom at an entrance, often just the snout and goggly eyes protruding. On seeing a diver it ducks back, then peers out for a second glance before disappearing into another chamber. Its diet is small fishes and crabs. It has a formidable array of sharp, conical teeth, and older specimens prey on much larger fishes. As it stalks across the bottom, its camouflage can be seen to alter rapidly from white dots to vertical dark bars to match the areas it is passing through. Over stones and sand, dots prevail; among weed and rocks the bars stand out. Within its lair the skin becomes so dark the patterns are obscure. While young grouper are rather shy and timid, adults show great curiosity towards divers. Since these grouper begin life as females, and later reverse sex, the large fishes are all males. At the Kermadec Islands, a marine reserve, there is a population of large spotted grouper. Divers have discovered they can play with these huge creatures. If a diver swims towards one, it may flee. But if ignored, the big fish may approach, even thrusting its head between two divers, touching both. If they tickle one under the gill plates and stomach, it relaxes totally, all colour draining away to near white. In this entranced state they can turn it upside down, rotate it end for end and pass it to and fro. If a fish disapproves of any action it may darken slightly. The spotted black grouper is found mostly in northern waters, around the North Island, but also off Westport.

Half-moon grouper *Epinephelus rivulatus* TL 35 cm

SERRANIDAE

W. Farrelly

This small subtropical grouper, light reddish to greenish brown, is patterned with six irregular brown bands of variable intensity and has a red-brown spot at the pectoral fin base. A carnivore of crabs and small fishes, it lurks under rock ledges by day and probably emerges to hunt at dusk. Even rarer is a similar species, *Epinephelus octofasciatus*, the convict cod, which has eight brown bars and reaches 60 cm. The species' distribution is confined to around north-eastern Northland.

Red-banded perch *Hypoplectrodes huntii* TL 20 cm

This is the most common and widespread of our small, solitary, bottom-dwelling groupers. It is home ranging in habitat; an individual has been observed resting passively in the same crevice for three years. On one occasion one was seen making repeated attempts to drive away a scorpionfish twice its size. The red-banded perch is restricted to New Zealand and is distributed right around the country. It is common inshore, but for some reason is not seen around the offshore Poor Knights Islands, where its smaller relative, the half-banded perch, is very abundant. Seven vertical bands of dark chocolate brown cover most of its body. There is no stripe through its eye. Its biology is probably similar to the half-banded perch. The red-banded perch feeds on crabs and small fishes. It is also known as banded perch.

Half-banded perch *Hypoplectrodes* sp. TL 15 cm

Most of the time this small grouper will be seen resting passively in a crevice. The usual time half-banded perch forage in the open is at dusk. When darkness falls they all return to their ledges. Sometimes they rest upside down beneath an overhang. Occasionally they fossick among kelp fronds for tiny mysid shrimps and other small crustaceans. In summer they steal eggs from the nests of demoiselles. Intensely territorial, they live at all depths down to 60 m, wherever they find a suitable recess. They have a home range of about 3 sq m. A density of eight fishes per 50 sq m has been found. Like many groupers, half-banded perch begin life as females and reverse sex to become males, usually after their second year. Naturally the males are bigger and there is a ratio of 2.7 males to each female. Solitary perch are usually males and it seems they may form breeding pairs, one large and one small. Spawning takes place in spring (September to December). Juveniles, miniature replicas of the adult, appear during January. They grow rapidly, reaching maturity in a year. Half-banded perch can be found in northern New Zealand to as far south as East Cape.

SERRANIDAE

Another small solitary species, the toadstool grouper was first discovered at the Poor Knights in 1969. As it stares from a crevice in the shallows during daylight hours, its brilliant, orange-red polkadot pattern, like an *Amanita* toadstool, has an obliterative effect in the dim light. At night its white spots change to dark blue, concentrated in vertical bands, and it prowls over the bottom in quick spurts, preying on small fishes and crustaceans with its fine, sharp teeth. Tiny, blue-dot triplefins are sometimes seen moving over the skin of a resting toadstool grouper, probably removing parasites, yet such fishes are normally part of the toadstool grouper's diet. In the Lord Howe Island lagoon, these grouper are very abundant everywhere, even beneath ledges just under the surface at the sea's edge. Toadstool grouper occur in northern New Zealand, mainly around offshore islands.

Pink maomao *Caprodon longimanus* TL 50 cm

Beneath the sea cliff, deep blue water suddenly glows neon pink with shapes weaving to and fro in a frenzy. A patch of water seethes with radiance for a moment. A school of pink maomao has chased its prey, tiny red euphausiid shrimps, up from the depths to the mirror of the surface, where escape is limited. Flexing their deeply forked tails and pivoting on especially long pectoral fins, the fishes wheel and turn, their upward tilted mouths snapping frantic prey with small, sharp teeth. Pink maomao mostly live where there is a moderate current, usually below the 10 m level. During the warmest months they frequently take refuge in the backs of caves where they appear to be asleep. Their bodies show the same white blotches as at night. At sunset, pink maomao schools stop feeding. Each night they return to roosting areas, moving in a long stream, to settle individually among the rocks before darkness closes in. Pink maomao actively seek cleanerfish to remove parasites, because while they have been feeding in dense plankton swarms, sea lice have fixed themselves to fin bases and near gill openings. The species is found around northern New Zealand to as far south as Hawke Bay.

Splendid perch *Callanthias australis* TL 30 cm

Splendid perch, female.

Much rarer, most exquisite and the deepest living of the plankton pickers, with larger fins and blunter head, splendid perch often swim in loose association with pink maomao, but only at levels beyond 30 m. At such depths, where colours are muted, it takes an experienced eye to distinguish their beauty; only when the electronic flash is fired does a living jewel glow for a split second. But colour is of importance to this species, and its eye must have some perception beyond our own. Lacking the subtle gradation of colours that make the male so exquisite (purple head, red-orange rear, yellow, purple-edged tail) the smaller female, around 20 cm, is a uniform orange-red, with purple-tinged fins and head. In late winter the males undergo a startling colour change: their bodies become latticed with a glowing mosaic pattern. The saffron-yellow patch near the tail disappears. The tail lobes become scarlet. The dorsal and anal fins are now incredibly marked with brilliant spots. Such a transition is puzzling. Then in mid-October the answer comes: a strange ritual takes place at a depth of 60 m, adjacent to the richly encrusted pinnacles and crags of the sea cliff. A school of some 30 splendid perch are rising and falling just above the rocks. Some are liveried in the bold lattice pattern, their gaudy fins widespread. Here and there these fishes are pairing with smaller ones in less attractive colouring. The gaudy fishes are the males, and the plainer ones, females. Often a female appears just above or below a male, as he pirouettes around her, displaying his dorsal and anal fins to make his body appear a third greater in depth. At times two or three males meet in an aggressive display, turning around one another as each fish demonstrates virility and majesty with imperious gestures, his body taut and curving. Then these males spiral up with one or two females, spawn and return to the school. No human ballet can surpass the expressiveness and finery of this undersea courtship dance. Splendid perch are distributed around northern New Zealand and as far south as Westport.

Splendid perch, male, normal coloration.

Splendid perch, male, courtship colours.

Butterfly perch *Caesioperca lepidoptera* TL 35 cm

As one of the plankton pickers, the butterfly perch has a similar lifestyle to the pink maomao, but it is not limited to plankton feeding: crabs and small shellfish also form part of its diet. This is probably why it has a smaller, deeper body (up to 30 cm) and, besides schooling in mid-water, it spends a lot of time swimming very close to the cliff face, oriented towards it rather than swimming horizontally. In a sea cave, butterfly perch often orient themselves to the roof, actually swimming upside down, which can make them difficult to photograph without the diver feeling dizzy. Probably because they select a different range of plankton animals, they are seldom seen pursuing prey up to the surface as do the pink maomao. Plankton feeding offers a variety of lifestyles and the members of this guild have adapted exquisitely to each variation in the food supply. At night, butterfly perch descend to the reef. A deeper red suffuses their skin and they nestle in the folds of a castle sponge, lie in holes or even swim very quietly, like somnambulists, just off the bottom. The species is found throughout New Zealand coastal waters.

Red-lined perch *Lepidoperca tasmanica* TL 20 cm

W. Farrelly

Divers mostly encounter this little-known deep-water species of small, carnivorous grouper on steep cliffs in Fiordland below 20 m. Distinctive are the multiple wavy orange-red stripes on its white body. The species occurs around the lower half of the South Island.

SERRANIDAE

W. Farrelly

Unlike the splendid perch of northern waters, its pinkish southern relative, the southern splendid perch, has only one colour phase. Their plankton-feeding lifestyles are similar. Distinctive are the yellow on its lower head and the graceful, trailing filaments on its tail. The species is found around the lower half of the South Island, at the Chathams and even at the remote Snares Islands. For the most part its schools are in depths beyond 25 m, but in Fiordland special features bring deep water conditions closer to the surface and the southern splendid perch is often within easy reach of divers.

Black rockfish *Acanthoclinus littoreus* TL 15 cm

In rock pools and estuaries, wherever it can find refuge in a crevice, beneath a rock or under a sunken log, the black rockfish hides, body braced so that its strong fins can wedge it in securely against wave turbulence or strong current. By night it preys on small invertebrates and fishes. Mottled black and olive, it has a distinctive white stripe on its head. In winter it spawns in a special nest chamber under a boulder where the male guards a ball of eggs until they hatch. Black rockfish is restricted to New Zealand and is widespread around the country.

CARANGIDAE

The kingfish is a roving carnivorous schoolfish that preys on demoiselles, koheru, and other plankton feeders. This lifestyle gives rise to its elliptical, streamlined form. Driven by rapid flexures of its rigid, V-shaped tail, the finely scaled, flexible body responds fluidly to a very powerful set of muscles. On attack it is a statement of beauty and strength. The fish's whole structure is involved. Such a high-energy burst requires extra oxygen use; mouth and gill flaps remain open for prolonged periods to increase water flow over the gills. An extra set of white muscles act as power boosters. To soar or dive through 70 m of ocean in less than a minute the kingfish needs an especially small swim bladder. As it descends, the gas-filled buoyancy organ is compressed and its body becomes a little heavier, but the pectoral fins act like the wings of a jet plane and give adequate lift to compensate. As a further aid to buoyancy the kingfish skull, like the body tissues, is full of oil, providing incompressible lift. The finely toothed jaws grasp prey and swallow it whole. The species is found around the North Island, and south of Cook Strait in summer. It is also known as yellowtail kingfish.

As a plankton feeder, the trevally has a deeper, more compressed body than its relative, the predatory kingfish. Lateral compression of the perfect cylindrical shape of pelagic fishes increases the surface area and adds to drag. The trevally sacrifices some speed for its compressed shape, but is much better adapted for its other roles: the vertical tilting action of plankton feeding and for bottom feeding. In summer trevally form close-packed schools, backs humping above the water as krill and other plankton are gulped down. Trevally are versatile and, when suitable plankton food is scarce, they forage on the bottom, sucking up sediment to sift out worms and other small organisms, before blowing the detritus out through their gills. As the trevally grows beyond 40 cm, its back becomes dark blue-green. Sharp, bony scutes on either side of the tail become more prominent and the head develops a hump. Such large adults abandon school feeding and forage in small groups around rocky headlands. Slow growing and long-lived, such fish may exceed 45 years. Juvenile trevally feed over reefs in small groups. Very small individuals, 2 cm long, sometimes remove parasites from other fish. The species is found around the North Island but summer stragglers reach to Banks Peninsula.

The koheru is a small, plankton-feeding schoolfish. Its near cylindrical, finely streamlined body is too short for it to have the speed of the longer kingfish. However, by dodging about in closely coordinated schools, koheru can usually elude predators. The yellow-green stripe on their flanks tends to merge the fishes together, making target selection difficult. In younger koheru more of the body surface has this yellow coloration, but it can be intensified or suppressed in a flash. When marauding kingfish move into sight, koheru will dodge down to the shelter of the reef, an unusual move for silvery, pelagic fishes. Koheru feed on smaller plankton animals than trevally do – mostly copepods – and they seldom school on the surface, preferring mid-water. As they mill around at high speed their flexible jaws extend intermittently to form a sucking tube. Juvenile koheru swim in much denser schools, often streaming up towards the surface and down to the reef in shimmering, silvery ropes. The koheru can easily be confused with the jack mackerel, *Trachurus novaezelandiae*, but with the latter its lateral line dips sharply midway along its length and its pectoral fins are so long they reach to the dip in the lateral line. Koheru can be found around northern New Zealand.

CARANGIDAE

W. Farrelly

Similar to koheru in most respects, greenish blue above and white below, the jack mackerel is distinguishable by the lateral line which dips sharply midway along its body; in addition, the longer pectoral fin extends to almost the same point. With growth the bony scutes along the lateral line become a prominent ridge. Juveniles in parking mode form erratic schools while juvenile koheru schools swim coherently. Jack mackerel is widely distributed throughout New Zealand waters, and is common in harbours and bays. It is also known as horse mackerel.

Whereas kingfish, trevally and koheru have flexible bodies, with fine, silvery scales, the arrow-like kahawai is covered with large, coarse scales that inhibit body flexing. Its main source of power is the broad tail and its rapid movements are more directed and unswerving. In its juvenile stages it is a plankton feeder; the adult is adapted to chasing small school fishes, yellow-eyed mullet, pilchards, piper and whitebait, as well as shrimps, krill and swimming crabs. Perhaps because such prey are more abundant in coastal waters, kahawai are only marginal around offshore islands such as the Poor Knights but form large schools inshore in summer when spawning takes place. When schools are feeding intensively their backs may break the surface, attracting seabirds. In winter they are more common in deeper, offshore waters. The kahawai can be very timid towards divers. Kahawai are prey for orca and bottlenose dolphin. The species is widespread around New Zealand.

SPARIDAE

As a wide-ranging carnivore that lives at all depths down to around 200 m, the snapper is an extremely adaptable fish with a broad feeding niche. Browsing on invertebrates, and even small fishes, its diet includes about 100 different species. When a certain food becomes scarce it has many alternatives. Crustaceans are generally the main food, especially crabs, and over reefs it finds great numbers of tiny sea urchins and tube worms. The snapper is a group-spawning fish. When surface water reaches 18°C in summer, schools aggregate in open water. Males become swarthy, almost black, and they rush around among the females, both sexes rising in groups to release eggs and sperm together. Over about four months repeated spawnings may occur, enhancing the possibility of success. Until their third or fourth year all snapper are females, then about half reverse sex to become males. Old snapper leave the school and often mooch around alone. The forehead develops a slight hump, the jaws and teeth strengthen, the skin becomes a uniform grey and they feed around the cliff faces in the shallows, prising loose large shellfish with their canine teeth. Snapper are mostly found in northern waters but stragglers reach south to Foveaux Strait.

Goatfish *Upeneichthys lineatus* TL 40 cm

Like a blind man dabbing his cane, the goatfish moves slowly over the bottom, its barbels flitting rapidly in front of its mouth, probing for tasty, soft-bodied invertebrates. A bottom grubber, it frequents sandy areas near reefs. The twin barbels hanging beneath its chin are well provided with sensitive taste buds. The mouth is protractile, angled downward, and the fish gulps its prey along with a fair amount of sand, which is expelled through the gills. The tiny teeth are unsuited to crushing shellfish or larger food, but can seize small fishes hiding on the sand. The goatfish has the chameleon ability to make lightning-quick changes of both colour and pattern. It is a keen patron of the cleanerfish. While being cleaned it may flush brilliant red, perhaps to render the skin parasites more visible by contrast. At night goatfishes rest in the open on sand, or under rock ledges. Now their bodies are pinkish, with darker red splotches, through which runs a red band along the lateral line. To maximise size, both dorsal fins are erect. Goatfishes mostly move about in loose schools varying from about five to 15 individuals of different sizes, seldom more than about 2 m above the bottom. Within kelp glades, they are more often seen swimming above the rocks and sand. They range in depth from the shallows down to 60 m. About twice as big as mature females, male goatfishes (17 cm) are seen in courtship colours during December and January, with a blue tinge to their bodies and fins. At this time, males establish breeding territories, repelling other males and courting females with elaborate displays of their handsome fins, and there are paired spawnings. The goatfish is present around New Zealand but is found mainly in North Island waters. It is also known as red mullet.

Black-spot goatfish *Parapeneus spilurus* TL 40 cm

Black-spot goatfish at night (lower).

Occasionally the black-spot goatfish, a tropical species, arrives in northern waters in larval form, transported by ocean currents. Some survive to maturity, but they do not seem to breed here. In the tropics they normally swim in schools. The herd instinct is so strong that migrant juveniles join up with any fish that will accept their company, mostly local goatfishes or a juvenile Sandager's wrasse. As they develop, they aggregate in small groups of their own kind. However, survival in this new world must be difficult: few reach full size. Black-spot goatfish is found in northern waters as far south as East Cape.

Bigeye *Pempheris adspersa* TL 15 cm

Bigeye, juvenile.

Beneath ledges, in the gloom of a cave or under a large rock, these gregarious little reef fishes swarm during the daylight hours, hovering in groups of a dozen and up to 150, heads to the light, darting to and fro as if afraid to venture out. Bigeye live at all depths, from 70 m to within 2 m of the surface, wherever suitable daytime refuge is available. Half an hour after sunset open water becomes alive with them; they flit about like beetles, or lie motionless in mid-water. By day they appear to be a dark, chocolate brown, but when illuminated at night, iridescent pink and purples appear. By starlight they feed on plankton. Easily confused with the slender roughy (p. 29), the bigeye is distinguished by its deeper, more compressed body, shorter-based dorsal and longer anal fin. Its eye, much larger, more than half the head length, is positioned directly above the mouth, which opens vertically like a trapdoor. In January, groups of juveniles, almost transparent green, appear. In daylight they school in kelp glades, swimming with a jerky motion, beating tiny, invisible pectoral fins. Bigeye are widespread around northern New Zealand waters as far south as East Cape.

The silver drummer is a chubby weed eater that prefers exposed, turbulent areas. For this reason it is a marginal species in areas where vertical cliff walls reflect waves with minimal disturbance. The drummer's powerful rudder-like tail can cope with the violent wave action, white water and fierce backlash that many fishes avoid. This adapts it to browsing on the fine brown and green algae and tender reds that grow profusely on wave-swept rocks, where tall, brown seaweeds find it difficult to anchor. A severe storm will strip off the finer seaweeds, but they grow fast and the rich supply of nutrients in exposed areas soon restores the sward once the seas moderate. Besides swimming in large herds over exposed, shallow reefs, silver drummers are often seen in small groups among rocks dashing about in great haste, dodging under ledges to hide for a while, then speeding to and fro for no apparent reason. They are seldom seen feeding, as they gorge themselves in rapid bouts at dawn and dusk. The juveniles live in the most turbulent, bubble-filled white water and are appropriately coloured: dark green with horizontal lines of light spots. The silver drummer is distributed throughout New Zealand waters. It is also known simply as drummer.

GIRELLIDAE

The powerful, deep-bodied bluefish spends a great deal of its time lurking under cover, especially among those heaps of tumbled rocks which form a maze of galleries and passages in shallow areas. Such apartments may shelter a dozen bluefishes of varying sizes, along with red moki and cave-dwelling fishes. The bluefishes come and go constantly, rarely staying still for more than a few minutes and seldom actually resting on the bottom. They seem to prefer areas where large expanses of shaded rock provide ideal feeding conditions. Their robust bodies and rudder-like tails adapt them well to the violent water motion that can afflict such a habitat. Closely related to the mado, the bluefish grazes encrusting life: shellfish, brittle stars, tube worms and crustaceans, as well as delicate red and green seaweeds, at dawn and dusk. Like its relative, the seaweed-grazing parore, it has tricuspid teeth, but in the bluefish these are set in several rows in each jaw. At times its brilliant blue body spotted with gold can darken rapidly to appear grey, almost black. Juvenile bluefish are similar to the adults, but are an even brighter blue with light spots. The bluefish is present in northern New Zealand and is also found around Kapiti Island.

Parore *Girella tricuspidata* TL 40 cm

Parore are wary, furtive herbivores, rather like wild sheep. In weedy, shallow bays they dart about in loose schools of up to 30. Rarely will they allow a diver within close range. As soon as one parore senses a movement, the whole group streams along the reef, keeping to the shallows. As they glide through a dappled kelp glade, the vertical bars on their silver-grey flanks disrupt the body outline. Feeding in a grove of bubble kelp their close-set, incisor-like teeth with three cusps shear off sections of brown frond with a sideswipe of the head. They crop the thin lawn of red algae up in the shallows and nip off blades of tender greens. Occasionally they gorge on pelagic salps in mid-water, their stomachs bulging with the gelatinous creatures. Parore mainly feed at dawn and dusk. At night schools break up and they rest in crevices alone, their bodies a dark brown, splotched with yellow. Juveniles, perfect replicas of the adults, often shelter close to the body of larger fish, only feeding when the protector pauses to graze; the adult often jerks its head as if in annoyance at its persistent mascot. The parore is found in northern waters to as far south as Cook Strait. It is also known as blackfish.

Blue maomao *Scorpis violaceus* TL 40 cm

Iridescent blue ellipses explode at the surface in a feeding frenzy. Myriad tiny pink euphausiid shrimps skip about with no hope of escape from the nimble blue maomao, foreheads humping above the surface, mouths slurping audibly, bodies as tightly packed as sardines in a can. Their V-shaped tails give them great dexterity; they can brake sharply with their pelvic fins, veer to either side with their pectorals and seize their planktonic prey individually with their small, finely toothed mouths, in much the same way as the fantail, an insect-eating bird, catches its prey. Of all the plankton pickers, these swim uppermost in the water column, seldom venturing below 20 m. At night blue maomao hover just clear of the bottom in rocky hollows, or cruise very slowly among the rocks. In summer, juveniles appear in small groups close to the rocks near the surface. Until they are about 10 cm long they have yellow anal fins and belly. A group of blue maomao will often dive-bomb a patch of sand among the rocks, skimming off it on their sides and ascending to await another turn. Blue maomao are present around north-eastern New Zealand with stragglers reaching south to Kaikoura and Golden Bay.

G. Edney

The sweep, a relative of the blue maomao, is amazingly similar to that species in almost every way except its colour, which is a uniform silvery grey. Sweep often school with blue maomao when plankton feeding. In south-east Australia they form large schools over reefs. In New Zealand, the sweep is present around the country but is more prevalent in northern waters.

Blue knifefish *Labracoglossa nitida* TL 20 cm

SCORPIDAE

G. Edney

Near the surface on the sea cliff among feeding schools of blue maomao and koheru small groups of blue knifefish dart about elusively, gulping at plankton. Bright blue, they have a flash of yellow from the tail to mid-body where it fades out. Another of the sporadic stragglers from subtropical waters, their numbers vary from year to year. The blue knifefish occurs in northern waters to as far south as East Cape, mostly around offshore islands and promontories.

Grey knifefish *Bathystethus cultratus* TL 30 cm

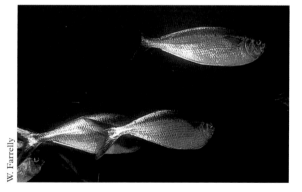

W. Farrelly

Grey knifefish resemble ellipses of living chrome as they huddle in the surge zone in a tight school or fan out loosely to feed on plankton. Their bodies are blue-grey with silver on flanks and bellies. A large school was once seen at the Mokohinau Islands but for the present they appear marginal in our waters. The species occurs in northern waters to as far south as the Bay of Plenty, mostly around promontories and offshore islands.

Dazzle-striped yellow and brown, the mado darts amid plankton-feeding fishes near the cliff face, but the species is a grazer of encrusting invertebrates. Mado are seen in the greatest numbers where there is a cave complex in the vicinity: masses of tumbled rocks or labyrinthine galleries. At such places, they swim in random schools down to depths of 40 m. In these shaded areas, expanses of rock surface are left bare of the larger seaweeds that depend on light, but encrusting animals thrive. The mado's diet consists of polychaete worms, anemones, and small amounts of hydroids, amphipods, shrimps and delicate red seaweeds. Juvenile mado act as cleanerfish. For a small mado, a crustacean parasitic on the skin of a fish would be just as acceptable as one crawling over a sponge. Juveniles up to 8 cm long have been seen cleaning demoiselles, blue maomao and the male red pigfish – even kingfish! In each case, the customer has to initiate the response with repeated posturings. Then the mado gives a dainty, desultory peck here and there, swimming off a little way until confronted again by the host fish, eager for attention. The mado occurs in northern waters to as far south as the Bay of Plenty.

Lord Howe coralfish *Amphichaetodon howensis* TL 25 cm

Almost always in a male-female pair, Lord Howe coralfishes, yellow with five black bands, live in or near sea caves and archways from 3 m down to 60 m. They prefer dim places supporting a rich growth of filter-feeding invertebrates. With its short, laterally compressed body the coralfish is extremely well adapted to manoeuvring around rocks and corals. The sharp dorsal spines, erected when alarmed, would make it virtually impossible for a predator to swallow. The mouth, at the end of a long snout, has tiny brush-like teeth for reaching into crevices for crustaceans, or nipping off the individual polyps from gorgonians, soft corals and other cnidarians. This specialised diet explains the limited habitat preference. On a coral reef, where the intensity of life is immense, brilliant coloration serves as a species-spacing mechanism to keep animals within territories or feeding ranges. Hence the aggressiveness of coralfishes, and the necessity for a male to form a permanent bond with a female and drive off others of its sex. At night the coralfish may be seen beneath rocks, fins erect, alert, with no change in coloration. The Lord Howe coralfish can be found in northern New Zealand waters to as far south as Mahia Peninsula.

Long-finned boarfish *Zanclistius elevatus* TL 30 cm

With its curving, translucent dorsal fin and slender snout, the long-finned boarfish has a dreamlike quality as it hovers near tubes of candelabra sponges. Because it lives at depths where the diver's senses are a little narcotised, this fish seems entranced and otherworldly as it glides slowly along the cliff wall in the sponge-dominated zone beyond 30 m. Besides its defensive value, the lofty dorsal fin gives the neutrally buoyant body great stability, like the keel of a yacht, enabling the protruding snout to be finely inserted among the branching and bulbous sponges to snap up brittle stars, worms and tiny crustaceans. The small, conical teeth are arranged in bands on both jaws, the outer row being enlarged and slightly curved. Long-finned boarfish are frequently solitary, yet are also often seen in pairs, probably male and female. Occasionally aggregations of up to 25 fishes have been sighted. The long-finned boarfish is present in waters around the North Island to as far south as Cook Strait.

Striped boarfish *Evistias acutirostris* TL 55 cm

A rare straggler from the subtropics where it lives in small groups, the striped boarfish is white with six dark brown bars: the first on its face; the second running onto the pelvic fin; all other fins are bright yellow. It is usually seen near shady archways where it probes for invertebrates with its long snout. The striped boarfish is present in northern waters to as far south as the Bay of Plenty.

Giant boarfish *Paristiopterus labiosus* TL 100 cm

W. Farrelly

A mysterious species not often seen by divers, although fishes may remain in the same reef area for long periods, often in a pair, one believed to be the male. The colour varies from grey to olive with dark, oblique markings and splotches. The supposed male often has pale markings on its flanks like scuffle injuries. Their long snouts probe mud and sand for prey animals, usually invertebrates. The giant boarfish is found in waters right around New Zealand, but it is probably more abundant in deeper waters. The species is also known as sowfish.

Kelpfish *Chironemus marmoratus* TL 35 cm

Mottled white and olive, this fish resembles a little grouper. It is quite gregarious and commonly lives in tribes of four to eight members, of varying sizes. The kelpfish lives in very shallow water, right up to the low tide mark and rarely beyond 25 m. Because this zone is subject to heavy wave action, the kelpfish must withstand severe buffeting and there are few fishes so well adapted to life in turbulent water. Its pectoral fins are so greatly developed they function like hands. Protruding rays can hook on to the bottom and the fins seem to clasp the rock. The kelpfish rests in narrow fissures or tunnels where water surges back and forth. It hugs the rock on every sort of incline, bracing itself with all fins, facing into the current. Diet includes many small marine animals: crabs, brittle stars, shellfish, worms and small blennies, which it hunts at first and final hours of light. As it lives in shallows, where light levels are high, its olive-brown, pepper-and-salt camouflage is perfectly adapted to merge with surroundings; this probably assists when stalking prey. Younger fish have a reddish tinge. The kelpfish is generally found in northern waters but stragglers reach Kaikoura. It is also known as hiwihiwi.

Marblefish *Aplodactylus arctidens* TL 60 cm

A heavy-bodied fish, the marblefish has the small, down-turned mouth of a weed eater. Its cryptic camouflage is well suited to the shallow kelp forest, where it lurks alone or in small groups. Seldom seen feeding, it prefers to graze on delicate brown or red seaweeds during the early morning and late evening. The body is well adapted to bottom grazing: triangular in cross section, with thick, fleshy pectoral fins for thrusting the fish along as it feeds like a lawn mower, clipping off the algal turf with tricuspid teeth. Concentrating on one type of weed at a time, it fills its capacious gut with small particles, which it spends most of its time digesting. During the day, it often rests at the entrance to a small cave. On seeing a diver, it rushes at him or her in a clumsy, lumbering tail drive, fins erect, body weaving sinuously, before veering aside and dashing back out of sight. Shortly after, it may make a second inspection before hiding altogether. Juveniles are olive green, while the adults are olive brown, marbled with white, varying in tone according to surroundings. The marblefish is common throughout New Zealand waters. It is also known as marble trout.

Notch-head marblefish *Aplodactylus etheridgii* TL 45 cm

The notch-head marblefish is easily confused with the common marblefish until the discerning eye notices some major differences: this subtropical species has a more slender body and does not grow as big. Most noticeable is the notch on its back where the head meets the body. While it has similar olive-brown coloration to its common relative, the notch-head marblefish has a pattern of small white spots and twin rows of larger white splotches. Around the edges of the gill flaps, eyes and mouth there are red tinges. Its lifestyle is similar to the weed-eating common marblefish but it does not behave in such a fussy, blundering manner. It is usually seen resting in a rocky refuge. The notch-head marblefish is present in northern New Zealand waters to as far south as the Coromandel Peninsula.

Red moki *Cheilodactylus spectabilis* TL 60 cm

Red moki are slow, home-ranging fishes living in small groups or alone wherever suitable shelter is offering. Females forage over shallow reefs down to 15 m. Beyond this depth, larger, deep-bodied males inhabit caves and tunnels, which they defend against rivals. During autumn, females visit these lairs at dusk to spawn. Males herd females into their territory, chasing and biting their tails if they try to leave. Red moki refuges seem to be permanent and they spend most of the daytime within them. Stray individuals may be seen foraging at any time, but most adults feed intensively for up to an hour at dawn and dusk, resting between meals. At night they remain alert in their shelters, dorsals erect to discourage predators, their body colours muted to a uniform brick red. Red moki have an extremely varied diet. Crustaceans are most important, including amphipods, isopods and crabs. Echinoderms eaten include sea urchins and brittle stars well hidden within the thick carpet of coralline red seaweed. At times the red moki eats enormous quantities of juvenile sea urchins; up to 60 have been counted in the gut of one small fish. Although it is seen munching away at the weed carpet, the red moki should not be mistaken for a herbivore. Feeding on encrusting limpets, small paua and chitons, the red moki reveals a special technique. Head

down-tilted, using its large pectorals to manoeuvre close to a rock, it bounces down with an audible clunk. Fleshy lips 'kiss' the food item off. Its jaws have bony plates of rasp-like teeth, which assist suction. This enables it to remove limpets, which teeth alone would not be able to prise loose. Its disruptive camouflage pattern (of eight irregular, vertical patches of brick red contrasting with white) breaks up the body contour as it moves among the stalks of a kelp forest or over a rocky reef. Very small juveniles are black and white. Large fishes, often uniformly brick red, may be 60 years old. Red moki are found in northern New Zealand waters, with stragglers reaching south to Foveaux Strait.

Painted moki *Cheilodactylus ephippium* TL 50 cm

Painted moki is a close relative of the red moki, but is more strikingly patterned with three oblique white bands and twin sets of protruding horns on its head. The painted moki lives close to areas of rock and kelp and has a similar lifestyle to that of the red moki. It is a straggler from the subtropics and can be found around northern New Zealand as far south as the Bay of Islands.

LATRIDAE

From the edge of the tide to depths of 60 m and beyond, porae glean the bottom for crabs, brittle stars, urchins, worms and shellfish. With their full, fleshy lips and in-turned teeth they nip off limpets and clumps of calcareous seaweed swarming with tiny animals. Their feeding style is similar to the red moki, but they range out over open sand, often kissing at a patch, filtering out any small creatures and ejecting the rest from their gills. While bottom feeding they use especially adapted, long pectoral fins as props, forming a tripod with the mouth. Their silvery blue colour varies from slate grey to tinges of gold on the upper body. Although usually seen as a solitary fish or in small groups, they sometimes congregate in large numbers. A resident tribe of up to 100 may live for many years in a deep, sandy arena. They are often seen resting out on the sand. At night, all fins erect, body blotched with a sleeping pattern, they hover on the bottom or wander through the kelp glades like sleepwalkers. Porae can be found around northern New Zealand and stragglers reach as far south as Kaikoura.

Tarakihi *Nemadactylus macropterus* TL 60 cm

The tarakihi has a broad diet similar to the snapper's, but it is more adapted to browsing invertebrates over fine, soft mud. Like its relative the porae, it poises its body at an angle propped on elongate pectorals, grubbing gently in mud or sand, adjusting its position with small fin movements. The tarakihi is really a deep-water fish, most abundant between depths of 50 and 200 m. Whereas snapper prefer warmer waters, inshore in summer and offshore in winter, tarakihi are the opposite: in summer their schools are most common from 100 to 200 m, and in winter from 50 to 100 m. The tarakihi may be confused with the porae, but it has several distinctive features: the black saddle on the head, shorter snout and thinner lips. Like the porae it has enlarged pectoral fins, the uppermost of the six rays very long, almost extending to the anal fin. The teeth are smaller and slender, forming velvety bands; the mouth is slightly down-turned. In their fourth to sixth year, at around 30 cm long, tarakihi mature. In autumn they migrate to spawning areas, especially off East Cape between Hicks Bay and Lottin Point (near East Cape) and in Fiordland. The tarakihi is widespread in New Zealand waters.

LATRIDAE

The blue moki is a school fish, distributed throughout New Zealand, but reaching its peak abundance in southern waters, with numbers tapering off in the Bay of Plenty. Only large individuals inhabit warmer northern waters, more usually seen at depths beyond 30 m, swimming over sand-floored canyons. In the south blue moki form schools of uniform-sized fishes, from juveniles to adults. After this they tend to swim in small groups of four to five or alone. While blue moki, especially juveniles, occasionally lurk beneath ledges and in caves, they are more commonly seen swimming over the sand in groups or schools near rocks in deeper water beyond 10 m, while smaller fishes live in the shallows, above 5 m. In South Island waters large schools of juveniles with dark green backs are seen around rocky reefs. Blue moki feed on small benthic animals; crabs, amphipods and other crustaceans predominate in their diet. The proportion of any one food no doubt reflects its availability and the local type of foraging ground. Small sea urchins, molluscs and errant polychaete worms are also taken. A large blue moki was seen feeding over a gravel bottom. Its body at a 45-degree angle with pectoral fins extended, it was grubbing gently with its thick, fleshy lips, nose down in the gravel, adjusting its position with small fin movements. These are wide-ranging fishes and have elongate bodies, V-shaped tails, relatively small pectoral and pelvic fins and are generally well adapted to an open-water mode of swimming. Their dorsal and anal fins are of much the same length. Off Gisborne and Lottin Point (near East Cape) in early spring blue moki from both north and south gather to spawn. The blue moki is also known simply as moki.

Copper moki *Latridopsis forsteri* TL 60 cm

LATRIDAE

W. Farrelly

Copper moki often swim with blue moki and while similar in form, lifestyle and diet, the body is dark olive green above, silvery below, with a thin, light yellow band along each row of scales. The rear edge of the tail has a distinctive black fringe. The copper moki is thinly distributed throughout New Zealand; it is rare in the north where it may swim with porae, and is most frequently seen around Stewart Island. It is also known as bastard trumpeter. Juvenile copper moki are more abundant in shallow inshore areas, the adults moving out to deeper waters. In Tasmania and other cool Australian waters the copper moki is much more abundant and migrates in very large schools.

LATRIDAE

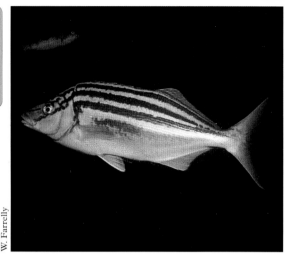

W. Farrelly

The trumpeter is a deep-water schoolfish. A basic yellow, its body has three dark longitudinal bands, which are continued on to the head in a series of dark blotches, and many bars. With their small, curved teeth trumpeter feed on crabs, shrimp, squid, octopus and small fish. The trumpeter is distributed throughout New Zealand waters but is rare north of East Cape. It often associates with blue moki and copper moki. These fishes were once quite common in commercial catches in the Cook Strait area and south to Stewart Island, where they are still prevalent. In 1891 they were reported in enormous quantities. Large numbers were once caught off Cape Saunders and Taiaroa Head, Otago, in depths of around 250 m and in deep water off Kaikoura Peninsula. In winter stragglers reach the Bay of Plenty and divers have sighted them around White Island. Something in the biology of this fish makes it particularly susceptible to decline in numbers due to commercial fishing pressure. The trumpeter is also known as kohikohi and Tasmanian trumpeter.

Single-spot demoiselle *Chromis hypsilepsis* TL 20 cm

The single-spot demoiselle is an Australian species with similar lifestyle that mixes with our endemic demoiselles and actually spawns here in the same spawning pattern. Demoiselles are mid-water feeders on plankton, mainly crustaceans. It can be found in northern waters to as far south as the Bay of Plenty, but densities of the species are very low. Single-spot demoiselle is yellowish green with a spot each side near the tail base.

Yellow demoiselle *Chromis fumea* TL 9 cm

W. Farrelly

Like the single-spot demoiselle this plankton-feeding damselfish has only one white spot each side but it is on the caudal peduncle. The juvenile, an intermittent larval traveller to our waters, has black margins on its tail and a distinctive yellow back with white lower half. This fades to a pale grey-blue with age and in the tropics, where mature adults abound, it is called the 'smoky puller'. Some years enough juveniles arrive to gather in small groups close to the reef, but they do not yet appear to survive the winter to reach adult form. The yellow demoiselle can be found around north-eastern Northland, especially around promontories and offshore islands, as well as in rocky estuaries.

81

Demoiselle *Chromis dispilus* TL 20 cm

Demoiselle, juvenile.

Demoiselles are the swallows of the sea. As plankton feeders, they are adapted to agile swooping and darting as they seize food carried on the current. Their broad pectoral fins act like sculls, boosting them forward after their prey of copepod crustaceans. In manoeuvring, their deeply forked swallow-tails open and close like scissors, giving the fishes perfect poise as they pivot in mid-water, small jaws and brush-like teeth snapping rapidly. With a large eye just above the mouth and only a single set of nostrils, these are highly visual animals. Twin dots on the flank are schooling signals and assist cohesion. In dense schools of up to 500, the demoiselles gain protection when kingfishes attack. The predator has difficulty selecting a single target from the mass of identical fish bodies and the myriad dots probably help confuse its aim. Demoiselles have a diet consisting almost entirely of copepods, small planktonic crustaceans that feed on plant plankton from the surface down to 70 m. Demoiselles rely on a moving mass of water for a steady supply of copepods. To obtain this moving water handy to the refuge of the reef, their schools face into the currents around rocky headlands, in archways, above pinnacles and alongside steep cliffs. In such areas eddy currents and turbulence concentrate the plankton swarms. Over the winter months, demoiselles tend to move deeper and their iridescent blue becomes a greyish blue tone. In June, at 70 m dense schools may be seen. In early spring, they often take refuge beneath ledges or roost in the fronds of sargassum weed like birds in a tree. During November they start to show an interest in rock surfaces. Schools break up and individuality asserts itself as males begin to prepare and guard nesting sites, their tails glowing with white streaks to attract females. From a schoolfish the demoiselle has become a fierce little aggressor, boldly guarding its chosen territory against all comers and, particularly, males of its own kind. For the next four months demoiselles spawn sporadically, and frequent hatchings of larval fishes enter the open-water plankton or leave to join other olive green juveniles sheltering beneath rock ledges. The demoiselle is found around the North Island, with stragglers reaching the Marlborough Sounds.

Demoiselle, adult male guarding nest.

Black angelfish *Parma alboscapularis* TL 28 cm

A plant grazer, the black angelfish does not range far for sustenance. Each fish hovers above its territory on the reef, centred on a ledge or crevice where it seeks refuge at night. It is a tiny ecological farmer working within its boundaries so that no weed patch is ever stripped bare or overgrazed. Short bouts

Black angelfish, juvenile.

of feeding are interspersed with turning and hovering, proclaiming its territorial rights. With such a diversified feeding pattern the sea plants can grow at least as fast as they are consumed; in this way the black angelfish is able to spend its entire life in one small area of shallow reef, down to 10 m. With the male there will be, somewhere within this territory, a jealously guarded nest site: a smooth, near-vertical patch of rock. Such a site is an asset that completely determines his reproductive success. Year after year he keeps it free from invading plants and encrusting animals, just allowing a close-cropped mat of red and green weeds to remain. In November spawning and nest guarding begins. One male may spawn with several females and there are often three or more overlapping circles of eggs of different colours, showing developmental stages. Within 10 days the eggs are all hatched. In January the

first babies appear. Initially the juvenile is chrome yellow with iridescent blue markings. A black spot ringed with blue appears on its dorsal fin: a false eye or ocellus to distract predators. Such bold coloration may also protect the young from the aggressiveness of parent fishes, which repel others of the species, yet allow juveniles to live within their territory.

Black angelfish adult, with juvenile Sandager's wrasse.

Over the ensuing 18 months the juvenile grows rapidly. The yellow fades to grey, the ocellus disappears, the blue lines lose intensity, the first dorsal fin increases in height and the body deepens. Throughout the juvenile period the fish inhabits the same small crevice in the shallows, seldom venturing out more than a few metres to feed. Amazingly, once it reaches adult size, there is no further growth for the rest of its life, which may extend for 50 years! Such is the premium on good nest sites that a young male may have to wait for another to die before he can spawn. Suitable nest sites seem to determine population densities. The black angelfish can be found in northern waters from North Cape south to East Cape.

Wrasses

Wrasses are mostly solitary fishes, which fossick over the reef using their sharp teeth to detach small invertebrate animals found on rock surfaces. They are characterised by their rat-like front teeth, thick lips and very flexible bodies. In the gullet there is a 'pharyngeal mill': upper and lower sets of grinding and cutting teeth in the throat, with which food is crushed before it enters the stomach.

Banded wrasse female, see p. 94.

Foxfish *Bodianus flavipinnis* TL 40 cm

At first sight a foxfish in its deep-water habitat looks like a red pig-fish but with *two* white patches on its back. However, its true colour, brought to life by the electronic flash, is a glowing orange-red, quite different from that of the red pigfish. Besides, it has sul-phur-yellow pectoral fins, a pure white abdomen, twin white patches on its back, and its head is convex and blunt. The foxfish has always been observed beyond 30 m, sometimes in pairs; it is likely the male and female forms are similar. Deep, closed-circuit divers see them swimming over the hull of the *Niagara* wreck, which lies on its side at 130 m, not far from the Poor Knights Islands. The foxfish is found in northern New Zealand waters as far south as Mahia Peninsula on the east coast and Cape Egmont on the west.

Elegant wrasse *Anampses elegans* TL 25 cm

Elegant wrasse, female.

At intervals of several years, gyres of warm water break away from tropical currents and bear down on New Zealand, bringing an influx of exotic species in larval form. Such was the case in the early 1970s, when five new wrasses were discovered at the Poor Knights Islands. Several times since then such influxes have occurred, with increasing frequency. These inner-space travellers settle out of the plankton on reaching a suitable habitat, and develop into females. Some survive several winters to become males and may even spawn. But eventually they die out, perhaps because winter temperatures fall below their level of tolerance. Such an arrival was the elegant wrasse, first discovered at Nursery Cove in February 1972 and subsequently found in both male and female forms. Young elegant wrasses, yellow with rows of blue dots, a grey mask between the eyes, move about in loose schools feeding rapidly in short bouts before speeding away to another site. The exquisitely coloured, gold-and-blue male is solitary, racing from group to group of females. These wrasses are common at Lord Howe Island, mid-Tasman, where so many species, marginal in our waters, abound. In New Zealand they are restricted to the far north and Poor Knights Islands.

Elegant wrasse, male.

85

Red pigfish *Bodianus unimaculatus* TL 50 cm

Red pigfish, female.

With its ruby-red body, an iridescent, blue-black ocellus on its imposing dorsal fin and a white patch towards the tail that intensifies as a signal when it is aroused, the male red pigfish is one of the most majestic of wrasses. Despite its beauty, the narrow, concave forehead and extended snout have led to its unflattering name. Undaunted by our label, the male red pigfish is a proud and boastful fish, patrolling its home range and displaying its fine livery to the females within its harem. The female red pigfish is a paler version of the male, but still very pretty. The ground colour of her body is pinkish white, with yellow on the abdomen overlaid with three rows of red dashes and 10 red lines. If the dashes are closely examined it will be noticed that each bears a 'signature' squiggle at the centre, varying with each fish like a bar code, and providing for individual recognition within the female dominance hierarchy. Juveniles are similar, but with a pure white ground and yellow fins. The male has a striking lunate tail, while the female's is truncate and the juvenile's gently rounded. Sex reversal occurs at around 30 cm in length. Red pigfishes range in depth from the shallows to 60 m, foraging for a wide variety of small invertebrates, their long, narrow jaws and sharp teeth being especially suited to extracting hard-shelled prey from narrow crevices: small shellfish, chitons, crabs, amphipods, brittle stars and ascidians. They even eat quite large sea urchins, a difficult prey, as it demands the breaking of many sharp spines to gain entry. At night the red pigfish rests in narrow crevices and tunnels, its fins erect and its colour unchanged. From July to September is their spawning time. Initially there is much sexual display and aggressive posturing. A male chases a female until she veers upwards. The two fishes ascend, belly to belly, gyrating and swerving. The male has his median fins erect and twists in a peculiar way until almost upside down. After rising some 6 m the pair spawn, part and return to the bottom to repeat the ritual. Occasionally a female may approach and court a male. Standing on her tail she sinks vertically before curving seductively around him, all fins elegantly displayed. Red pigfish can be found in northern waters as far south as East Cape.

Red pigfish, male.

Girdled wrasse *Notolabrus cinctus* TL 35 cm

At first encounter the girdled wrasse is easily mistaken for a spotty (p. 92), although it grows about one-third bigger. Unlike the spotty it has just two growth stages: juveniles and adults. There are no visible gender differences. Juveniles are olive-brown with a pale band mid-body. With adults this band becomes a blue-grey girdle on a brown-grey body. Divers mainly encounter this deeper water wrasse at Stewart Island and in Fiordland, but they have been seen at Coromandel and the Three Kings Islands. The species generally

W. Farrelly

occurs mostly in southern waters, with stragglers reaching these northern places, probably via the west coast. They feed on shellfish, crabs and other crustaceans including planktonic animals. Juveniles remove parasites from fish. At Stewart Island divers have become wary of girdled wrasses because they approach curiously and bite the diver's lips with rat-like teeth. A bristly moustache provides defence.

87

Sandager's wrasse *Coris sandageri* TL 45 cm

Sandager's wrasse, juvenile.

Of all our fishes the Sandager's wrasse is the most markedly polymorphic: juveniles, females and males are quite different in colour
and form. Even transitional stages between each growth phase can
be clearly recognised. The slender juveniles are boldly emblazoned with the advertising emblem of a fish cleaner: a white body
with a golden-yellow median stripe and a significant black dot at
the tail base. When the juvenile reaches around 15 cm, transition
to female form begins. The yellow band takes on a russet tinge and
gradually separates in the middle. The body then deepens and
eventually the two portions of the broken band become salmon-
coloured patches on a white body. The black dot at the tail base
fades away: the fish has become a mature female. Females of varying sizes fossick for invertebrates over rock faces and across the
sand at the foot of the undersea cliff in loose aggregations of from
10 to 20, accompanied by similar numbers of juveniles at all stages
of growth. These females are not part of any male harem, but wander freely through all territories. Somewhere on the fringe of the
group will be a deep-bodied, blunt-headed male. An extremely
handsome fish, his grape-coloured body is embellished with a
multi-coloured saddle: alternating pairs of white and deep
maroon bands, a wedge of saffron yellow, a red pectoral base and
mauve cheeks. These proclaim his masculinity to the females in his
area and to all other males. No male can enter his territory without provoking a vigorous aggressive display, although injuries are
seldom inflicted. The pattern of the saddle colours varies with
individuals, and this plays an important role in the community:
each male is instantly recognisable, even to other species. Since all
Sandager's wrasses commence life as females, there are no young
males. Among a group of females there is a hierarchy or pecking
order maintained by daily contact and individual recognition.
With the death of the male, the dominant female in any group is
released from male dominance. In response to male hormones
then released in her body she undergoes a sex change and replaces
the male within two weeks. Spawning is from December to March
when there are frequent sexual displays and aggressive pursuits.
The male parades around his territory, erecting his fins to accen-
tuate body size and masculinity. If he comes across a female ready
to spawn, the typical wrasse-style spawning ascent occurs. Divers

Sandager's wrasse, female.

were amazed to discover how these fish spend the night. As daylight fades they gradually localise movements until small groups hover over sand patches. With the last squibs of light they vanish beneath the sand. Last to go to bed is the male. These fishes are adapted to wriggling on their sides under sand. Unlike many other wrasses they have small scales and very flexible bodies. Their gills pump a sufficient flow of water through sand particles to support a resting fish. Diet includes most of the small animals that encrust rocks or live in crevices, especially brittle stars, amphipods, chitons and gastropods, along with limpets, bivalves, polychaete worms and small crabs. For the juveniles, parasites are not the major source of food. They fossick after small bottom-living organisms, which they nip daintily off the rocks. They mainly clean demoiselles, but also blue maomao, parore, black angelfishes, goatfishes, spotties, banded wrasses, porae and koheru. Once one was seen to enter the mouth of a goatfish, rip out a large sea louse and dash it against a rock until dead, before swallowing it. Sandager's wrasse is present in northern waters, to as far south as East Cape.

Sandager's wrasse, male.

Combfish *Coris picta* TL 22 cm

Combfish, female.

The combfish is a fish cleaner, closely related to the Sandager's wrasse. A small, specialised cleaner, it never grows beyond suitable proportions for this role. It bears very prominently the advertising emblem for a parasite picker: a chocolate-black median stripe, scalloped or comb-shaped along the lower edge. There is also a short red stripe along the head in front of the dorsal fin. With juveniles, the black median stripe extends right to the end of the tail. At maturity (about 8 cm) the combfish develops a beautiful golden yellow tail, which contrasts with the body to make this little fish even more conspicuous as it sculls along, lazily beating its transparent pectoral fins. These are home-ranging fishes and have been observed in the same place for many months. Such areas become recognised by the other reef fishes as 'cleaning stations'. Typically they are in rocky areas, close to sand, under which the combfish spends the night like the related Sandager's wrasse. Cleaning intensity varies from day to day. On one occasion, a combfish was seen to clean 16 fishes in a 54-minute period within an area no larger than a small house. As it moved about its home range it was completely preoccupied with cleaning and sought out fish after fish, pecking at fin bases, gill covers and mouths. It spent five minutes with a goatfish, pecking at it 50 times. This goatfish was initially vermilion; it paled to white and then flushed vermilion again, perhaps to make parasites in various areas stand out in contrast. The combfish then cleaned some demoiselles with six pecks each; then two porae, a male orange wrasse and a male Sandager's wrasse. While being attended the demoiselles were poised in a rosette, all focused on the cleaner, fins extended, as the little fish wove to and fro among its customers. The male combfish looks exactly like the female but during courtship or aggression a startling transformation occurs. The black stripe vanishes! The back is now blue-grey; through its eye and curving down along the gill edge is a chocolate-black crescent; the belly is yellow-brown and the tips of the pectorals are dark blue. The combfish is a subtropical species, abundant at Lord Howe Island and only a sporadic coloniser in our northern waters, especially around promontories and offshore islands. With climate change it may become established here.

Combfish, male.

Spotty *Notolabrus celidotus* TL 26 cm

Spotty, female.

Like the humble house sparrow, the spotty is one of the most widespread and nondescript of the wrasse family, yet it has a complex society. Spotty populations reach high densities over shallow inshore reef flats, around harbour wharves and in tidal rivers. The broad distribution is matched by its range of diet. One of the least discriminating wrasses, the spotty fossicks with its sharp little teeth for small shellfish, crabs, hermit crabs and, to a lesser extent, amphipods, shrimps, barnacles, chitons and polychaete worms. The female varies in colour from yellowish green to pale greyish white to brown, but her body bears a regular series of four dark bars and a bold black blotch. On the yellow anal fin are two black dots. Juveniles settle out of the plankton between December and February. Sheltering close to the kelp forest, they swim in loose, foraging schools, but space out as they grow and eventually fossick in a solitary fashion, each within its own small territory. Females mature in the August of their first or second year, depending on their growth rate. When females reach around 16 cm, in their third or fourth year, most change sex as soon as the spawning season is complete. With the male, vertical bars and fin dots vanish. The black blotch stretches into a pattern of black spots. The gill plates are patterned with blue lines and each fawn scale on his body bears a tiny spot of blue. Males tend to live in deeper water than females, and some older ones are able to control a territory from which they repel other males: these are the most successful breeders. Spawning takes place from late July to early December, when females move to deeper areas and males chase them on to their courtship grounds. There the male circles the female, signalling with his dorsal. If she is ready they come together on the bottom and dash upward, almost touching. Increasing pressure on their swim bladders forces out twin clouds of eggs and sperm which mingle as the fishes veer aside and descend. Larval spotties spend two months wandering in the plankton before settling to the bottom and developing pigmentation to suit their environment. Those among sea lettuce are lime green. At night the spotty rests on the bottom, sheathed in a protective mucus envelope, all markings faded. The spotty is restricted to New Zealand and is widespread around the country. It is also called kelpie, guffy and paketi.

Spotty, male.

LABRIDAE

Banded wrasse, female.

A wide-ranging species, distributed all around New Zealand, the banded wrasse lives much closer to the kelp forest than the spotty, and its colours provide good camouflage. It is a more selective fossicker, with a distinct preference for small, hard-shelled animals: crabs, hermits, limpets, chitons, small paua, mussels, topshells and baby sea urchins, found in crevices, in seaweed holdfasts and amid encrusting growths, where it forages with especially prominent, rake-like teeth. Amid weedy shallows lurks the shy juvenile which varies in colour from light purple to redbrown and mottled brownish green. Along its back and extending on to the dorsal fin, it has a series of six bright dots. As it matures into the olive-green female, these dots become yellowish-green wedges of colour. With transition to the male, the wedges extend more and more on to the body, along with a matching series along the base of the anal fin. Eventually the ground colour of the body breaks up into six dark purple, equally spaced vertical bands. The male has a blunter head and deeper body. It tends to live in deeper water than the female, down to 30 m. While most wrasses begin life as females, reversing sex upon reaching a certain size, banded wrasses are not consistent with this pattern. Many actually start life as males. Once development from the larval stage is complete, others may change from female to male at any time. Those that make the transition while young will never function as spawning females. On the other hand, some continue as females all their lives – more than 25 years. These 'super females' grow as large as mature males. Although they still retain their green female coloration, matrons develop the deep body and blunt head of a male, and its extremely prominent teeth. Since almost half a population of banded wrasses are males, competition among a relatively large number of males is intense. During the winter spawning season, from August to September, divers often see males hotly pursuing females, all fins raised, yellow markings gleaming brightly during the chase, while the female's drab colour is unchanged. By day banded wrasses are continuously on the move, but about an hour before sunset they vanish. By night they rest in crevices. The body has a peculiar, furry appearance, enclosed in a sheath of mucus exuded from special skin glands to provide a protective envelope.

Banded wrasse, male.

Green wrasse *Notolabrus inscriptus* TL 60 cm

Green wrasse, female.

Another subtropical visitor, the green wrasse does not yet seem to breed successfully in our waters, but arrives as a larval fish from the reefs to the north. This may change with global warming. It is a very large and handsome wrasse. Its diet is mainly shellfish and small crustaceans. There are three distinct phases of growth. The juvenile is brown-green with a green-tinged head and 10 horizontal bands of silvery yellow dots along its sides. The female is dark brown and develops a pretty 'scribbled' scale pattern of horizontal lines and vertical squiggles. The male is a most impressive fish, with a powerful, blunt head and elongate, wedge-shaped body. He is dark olive green with boldly contrasting light yellow dorsal and anal fins, which are used for aggressive and sexual displays. At the base of the leading dorsal spine there is a prominent black dot, only visible when the fin is erect, in a signal mode. Females and juveniles lurk among the seaweed fronds and are well camouflaged, while the males swim boldly in the open near the weed. These are home-ranging fishes and in July, during their spawning

Green wrasse, male.

season, a male may be seen to chase a rival from near the surface down to 50 m and beyond. All fins are erect like gleaming banners, maximising the size of the attacker and signalling his aggressiveness. Not all females reverse sex and some continue to grow, with female form and colour, into huge maiden aunts, or super females. One of these, whom divers called 'Lola', became very friendly and curious. For many years Lola was regularly encountered in the same small area of reef, seemingly lolling in clownish ecstasy among the kelp fronds. With her body at an oblique angle she fell slowly, then wriggled, rose, and repeated the stance: 'Lola the circus fat-lady'. In this state she showed no fear and divers could observe her as close as they wished. But when a woman was looking at her at very close range, a sudden disturbance sent Lola hurtling into her arm in blind panic, gouging the wet suit rubber with her large canines. Poor Lola! The green wrasse is found in northern waters as far south as East Cape, mainly around promontories and offshore islands.

Orange wrasse *Pseudolabrus luculentus* TL 25 cm

Orange wrasse, female.

In May, off the end of a long reef a group of 30 male orange wrasses are hovering above the kelp forest, circling and sparring intermittently with each other. Beneath, among the kelp stalks, are similar numbers of females. From time to time four or five females soar up into the male throng; if the males are not receptive they chase the females down again. Occasionally a male courts a female, both fishes arching around each other tensely, all fins erect. Then rapidly, with eel-like, sinuous swimming movements, the pair ascend side by side about 3 m, before turning and releasing twin clouds of eggs and sperm. Both fishes then rejoin their groups. This pattern is often varied by group spawning movements, when one or two others accompany the spawning couple in their upward rush and all the fishes spawn together. Such group spawnings by orange wrasses have been observed in the same location throughout their unusually long spawning season (March to October) and for year after year. Later in the season, paired spawnings similar to those of other wrasses also occur. The double spawning pattern ensures a wider distribution of spawn, which increases their chances of survival. The orange wrasse is a

Orange wrasse, male.

subtropical species that has adapted well to the kelp forests of northern New Zealand. Juvenile and female fishes are a brilliant apricot orange. Gill covers bear silvery cheek straps that continue along the body as five rows of white-flecked scales. Six vertical white bands may also be apparent, but they vary in intensity. At around 15 cm in length, females become males. The male has a much deeper body, brick red to mauve with a chequerboard pattern of four black and five white squares on his back extending partly on to his dorsal fin, and a splatter of red dots on his green-tinged cheeks. During courtship and aggression, this chequerboard pattern gleams with signal intensity. All phases have a dot at the pectoral base, black in the female, teal blue in the male. There is another colour form, in which the adult has a handsome green head, but no chequerboard pattern; this is either a transitional stage going towards the male, or else a super female. Orange wrasses feed on small crustaceans. Small females supplement their diet as fish cleaners, attending to porae, blue maomao and black angelfishes. The orange wrasse is found in northern New Zealand waters.

Scarlet wrasse *Pseudolabrus miles* TL 40 cm

Scarlet wrasse, female.

The depth range of the scarlet wrasse seems to begin where that of the spotty and banded wrasse tapers off. Seen mostly below the 10 m level, these sumptuously coloured fishes are among the few wrasses observed beyond 60 m. Both the red coloration and the diet of these fishes are adapted to a deeper range and to bottom-fossicking habits. They have a strong preference for hermit crabs, along with brittle stars, small urchins and shellfish. Densities of these wrasses are much greater in cooler waters where aggregations of several fishes in every square metre may be seen, as in Fiordland. As a diver swims over a reef, a scarlet wrasse will occasionally follow him or her. Entering the territories of others of its species, it suffers furious attacks, but still continues in the diver's wake. The diver can observe that these fish patrol territory borders and swim along regular and predictable pathways. Their course is rather like a clockwork train: over a ridge, around a rock, between two kelp thickets and along a sand-floored canyon. Sometimes very large males rest within deep recesses during the day – most unusual for a wrasse. There are three growth phases. The slender, orange-red juvenile is like the female, in that both have rows of red and yellow scales on the lower part of the body. The female is a brighter red and loses the three pale spots that the juvenile bears on its back. In about the third or fourth year, after at least two seasons as mature,

Scarlet wrasse, male.

functional females, sex reversal occurs and the females become males. At all stages there is a distinctive black wedge at the tail base. Male scarlet wrasses have a deep body and blunt head, while the tail becomes markedly lunate with extended lobes. The multiple red and yellow stripes on the belly of the female are replaced by a uniform red, often with a salmon-pink cast. During winter courtship takes place and there are bold fin displays and vigorous pursuits. This is one of the most aggressive wrasses and will nip a rival viciously with its sharp teeth. In spring the male has been seen courting and spawning with a group of females. The scarlet wrasse is restricted to New Zealand, where it is widespread around the country, but more prevalent in the south. It is also known as soldier.

Rainbowfish *Suezichthys arquatus* TL 18 cm

Rainbowfish, female.

Under water, where light is muted, the female rainbow fish appears red-pink with 10 horizontal blue stripes. Most noticeable are the three black dots on her fins: one near the front of her dorsal, another near its rear; a third is at the base of the tail, above the midline. With wrasses, such dots seem to have a signal function, perhaps assisting species recognition on a busy reef. Larger than the female, at first glance the male is a bluish coloured fish, and retains only one of the fin dots, that at the front of the dorsal fin. Most distinctive is the strangely shaped and elaborately patterned tail, semi-lunate, the upper lobe extending almost to a thread. For sexual or aggressive signalling this tail is virtually a flag, the upper third a brilliant yellow, the lower part a burgundy red. His back is dark green with a burgundy-tinged abdomen, overlaid with 10 rows of bright blue dots, the upper rows coalescing to form continuous stripes. Dorsal and anal fins are rich burgundy red, with blue and green patterning. This is among the most intricately patterned and brilliantly hued fishes in New Zealand seas. Rainbowfishes usually swim in male/female pairs, rare for wrasses, and they live within the same small territory all their lives. Pair formation may begin soon after the fishes settle from the plankton. Then, after about a year's growth, the larger of the two fish reverses sex to become the male. Spawning is in winter. Where the seafloor meets the kelp forest, a male rainbow fish swims just above the white sand. He approaches the female, spreads median fins slightly, and undulates horizontally alongside. Six times he repeats this ritual, approaching each time from behind, and afterwards swimming away about 2 m before returning. On the last two occasions he becomes very agitated and pecks her flanks. She then spreads her median fins, and very swiftly they both swim upwards, bellies almost together. A metre up they part. As they turn they shoot out little white clouds of eggs and sperm, which intermingle and disperse. They then return rapidly to the bottom and the male moves off. An immigrant from the subtropics, the rainbowfish was first sighted at the Poor Knights Islands in August 1971, and successive invasions have persisted longer and longer to the point where it may well have become established here. It is found in northern waters to as far south as the Bay of Plenty.

Rainbowfish, male.

Crimson cleanerfish *Suezichthys aylingi* TL 15 cm

Crimson cleanerfish, female.

The crimson spindle of his body emblazoned with a radiant white stripe, the male crimson cleanerfish is a most conspicuous fish. His violet chinstraps, elaborate scale flecks and fin markings, and bright orange tail boldly proclaim male status. The white stripe advertises his parasite-picking role, attracting client fishes from afar and inhibiting potential predators, which recognise him as a groom rather than a meal. The female is a little less obvious, being orange with a white flash extending from the mouth and merging midway along the body into the general colour pattern. Her fins are translucent and she has a black distinguishing dot near the end of her dorsal fin. The juvenile resembles the female, but being very small it is quite inconspicuous, even when present in great numbers just above or within the kelp forest. Life begins at the outset of the year when tiny juveniles just over a centimetre long settle out of the plankton. After about seven months, at 7 cm, they mature and, for the next one to two years, live as females, courted by harem-keeping males in small, heavily guarded territories. Then, in February or March, a mass sex change occurs. At first, large numbers of very small males form small groups, fighting with each other, raising their dorsals in threat display and circling pugnaciously. Nearby is a small male with a black dot on the rear of its dorsal – the distinctive marking of a female! While its body is a pale red it still bears the faint vertical bands of a female. It also has the continuous white stripe of a male. This is a male fish in a state of transition from the female form. Sex reversal is surprisingly rapid: only one to two weeks for both the outward colour change and internal conversion from ovary to gonad. Fighting, among newly transformed males, occurs while they are establishing territories. But within three days new boundaries have been defined, each male patrolling a tiny patch and cleaning other fishes. Several months of warring follow during which many young males die, so that the stronger fishes gradually accumulate bigger territories and more females. By the time spawning commences in June, everything has been sorted out and many of the old-established males have died. The crimson cleanerfish has a lifespan of four years and is found in northern waters to as far south as East Cape.

Crimson cleanerfish, male.

Moon wrasse *Thalassoma lunare* TL 25 cm

Moon wrasse, female.

A subtropical straggler that has made several attempts to establish here at long intervals, the moon wrasse never seems to get past the second phase of development when it becomes apparent to divers. Never sighted, the tiny juvenile must be exceedingly secretive. It has a bright blue lower body, green head with irregular pink eye stripes, black spots mid dorsal and at the tail base, and about six white patches along the dorsum. This develops into the female with green body, blue head with pink eye stripes and blue-edged; the pink-banded tail lobes have a central yellow patch. The juvenile spots and patches disappear. The handsome male is a turquoise blue with pink head stripes, blue and pink trim along dorsal and anal fins, and on the pectorals and tail lobes, which retain the central bright yellow patch. As yet no female has persisted long enough in New Zealand waters to develop to this final stage, but with climate change very handsome male wrasses like this and those on the following pages may appear. The moon wrasse is found in northern waters around offshore islands.

Long green wrasse *Pseudojuloides elongatus* TL 15 cm

As subtropical stragglers these are highly secretive wrasses that move around in kelp beds to 20 m. In the subtropics they form aggregations, usually with one very active male. Juveniles vary from brown to green according to habitat. Adults develop bright blue markings on head and fins. The long green wrasse can be found in northern New Zealand waters around offshore islands.

Sunset wrasse *Thalassoma lutescens* TL 25 cm

R. Armstrong

Sunset wrasse, juvenile.

Juveniles of this subtropical straggler are seen here in spring but few appear to survive the ensuing winter. Juveniles, up to 5 cm, are green-yellow with a dark median stripe terminating in a black dot; the belly is white. When they develop into adults, likely to happen more often with climate change, they are golden yellow with pale red stripes behind the eye; they have blue-tipped pectorals. Males are splendid with a green-striped, pink head, a turquoise to green body and a pink-striped tail. The sunset wrasse juveniles can be found in northern New Zealand waters around offshore islands.

Butterfish *Odax pullus* TL 75 cm

Butterfish, juvenile.

Among writhing blades of kelp, dark shadows weave and glide. Fins like streamers undulate in the thresh and ply of surges with a silent beauty only a seaweed forest can offer. In this fluctuating world the herbivorous butterfish blends so perfectly as to vanish before the eyes, melting into a loose scrap of weed. Butterfishes browse on erect, canopy-forming seaweeds. Teeth fused into bony ridges, they mouth tender fronds, nip out a disc and macerate it with the grinding teeth in their throats. They have a long spawning season, commencing early July and ending late February. Over this eight-month period, spawning takes place several times. On exposed rocky shores, subject to heavy storms, extended partial spawning is an adaptation to ensure survival of eggs. Many reef fishes in temperate zones share this strategy, so that larval development and early growth take place in summer. Outside the spawning season, males mostly live in depths beyond 10 m, while females and juveniles inhabit the shallows. Called 'disjunctive sex distribution', this spreads the range of feeding and leaves the most tender food sources for younger fishes. During the spawning period, both sexes exhibit a violet-blue chinstrap on the lower jaws, and blue dots and whorls on the gill flaps. Those of the male are more splendid and he bears similar markings on his elongate anal and dorsal fins. Males establish territories, repelling other males and courting females by using bold fin displays. Over the months prior to spawning, females build up a store of fat in the intestine. Juveniles go through three colour phases: very small, slender butterfishes are red-brown, with a pale median stripe. Extremely shy, they seldom leave the shelter of the kelp forest. As they grow, butterfishes become a rich golden brown. By this stage they are more active and often group together above the weed canopy. Adults undergo three more distinct colour changes. By the time they reach 45 cm, most have taken on the final colour pattern: the back is very dark, almost black; the median stripe, a series of lighter patches. Melding in and out of vision they move sinuously, sculling their pectorals and undulating dorsal and anal fins, only using the tail for sudden bursts. All butterfishes begin life as females. In the fifth or sixth year sex reversal occurs and females transform into males, in a ratio of two to one. The butterfish is restricted to New Zealand, and is widespread, especially in the south. It is also known as greenbone, for the bone colour.

Butterfish, male.

Thornfish *Bovichtus variegatus* TL 25 cm

R. Armstrong

A small lurking carnivore of tide pools and exposed shallow reefs, the thornfish is greatly variable in colour from red to green or black, with paler mottlings. Its fins are often yellow with lines of dark spots. There is a distinctive sharp spine on the rear edge of its gill cover. Its diet is seafloor invertebrates, mainly crustaceans. The thornfish is related to the fishes of Antarctic waters and another species of thornfish occurs in southern Australia. The thornfish occurs mostly in the Wellington area and around the South Island to New Zealand's subantarctic islands.

W. Farrelly

Fifty metres down on the white sand at the foot of a cliff, the diver sees something odd among the coral rubble. A gentle prod and hey presto! A weird, fat-headed fish with tapering body emerges in a flurry and settles on the sand nearby. Its huge, armour-plated head, bristling with sharp spines, houses an upward-gaping, cavernous mouth. Right on top of the flattened skull, its eyes command an all-round view. With pectoral fins like small wings and a pumping action of the broad gill flaps it can rapidly fan its way down into the sand until only the eyes and a faint suggestion of jaws remain visible. Should a fish or crab wander by, the trapdoor opens and the grotesque monster surges up to engulf its prey. Giant stargazers can reach almost a metre in length and their capacious jaws can accommodate fishes almost half their own size. The species is restricted to New Zealand, and is more abundant in southern waters to depths of 500 m. The giant stargazer is also known as monkfish.

Giant banded stargazer *Kathetostoma* species

URANOSCOPIDAE

Scientists are still investigating this brownish grey, dark-banded species of giant stargazer which divers have been seeing occasionally at the Poor Knights Islands. It may prove to be *Kathetostoma laeve* of south-east Australian waters which reaches a total length of 75 cm. The distribution of this curious species in New Zealand has yet to be determined.

Spotted stargazer *Genyagnus monopterygius* TL 45 cm

R. Armstrong

A smaller species, the spotted stargazer, sometimes called a 'toe-biter', lives inshore to 100 m and in estuaries and harbours. Green-brown to grey above, white below, covered with large creamy white oval spots, it has a small, distinctive barbel under its chin. Because it is normally buried in sand or mud, with just the top of its head emerging, to ambush crabs and small fishes, divers are more likely to find it at night. The spotted stargazer is restricted to New Zealand and is widespread.

Opalfish *Hemerocoetes monopterygius* TL 25 cm

PERCOPHIDAE

Q. Bennett

While widespread around New Zealand in deeper waters to around 200 m on mud or sand, the opalfish is more likely to be within diver range in Fiordland. It has a pointed snout, flattened head, somewhat upward-looking eyes, and a long, colourful dorsal fin on a slender body. The pale brown body, patched with white saddles, is adorned with iridescent blue and orange markings on head and flanks. Its diet is crabs, shrimps and small fishes. The opalfish is restricted to New Zealand.

W. Farrelly

Blue cod *Parapercis colias* TL 60 cm

W. Farrelly

Blue cod, female.

Throughout New Zealand, from the Three Kings Islands to Stewart Island, the inquisitive blue cod glides up over sand or low flat rocks, poises on its strong pelvic fins and goggles at the diver. It will playfully nip fingers and gradually become so friendly as to allow the diver to stroke its head. When swimming it uses its pectorals, as the tail fin is kept folded except for fast bursts. With its pelvic fins in advance of the pectorals and its cylindrical body, the blue cod is well adapted as a bottom-dwelling fish. Not really a cod at all, it belongs to a group of tropical species, the weevers. There is a marked territoriality. Individuals stay in the same area all year round and, from their familiarity with the diver, show a remarkable degree of memory. The blue cod lives down to 100 m in areas of rocky bottom, with patches of sand and weed. It is a voracious carnivore and eats a very wide range of marine animals: pilchards, sprats, seahorses, pipefishes, mullet, blennies, sea perch, red pigfishes, rock cod and spotty; nine species of mollusc, eight types of crustaceans (including four crab species) and five species of marine worms. The soft-shell crayfish has been found in the stomach of a large blue cod. Chatham Island specimens have been found full of pelagic salps. The blue cod has only small teeth in the jaws, but the roof of the mouth and the throat are lined with sharp, strong teeth, like a coarse wood rasp. As it swallows, prey is seized and crushed in these teeth as the powerful gullet muscles contract. Females are darker with brownish white marbling.

Blue cod, male.

Young males may be this colour too but large blue cod that are blue with greenish heads are likely to be male. In autumn tiny juveniles, white with twin black stripes, may be seen darting about. The blue cod is restricted to New Zealand and is widespread around the coasts, although more abundant in the south.

Red-banded weever *Parapercis binivirgata* TL 18 cm

At depths beyond 60 m at the Poor Knights Islands, further down than most divers would venture without closed-circuit scuba gear, one tiny fish may be very abundant over the sand. In some areas every small patch of rubble is claimed by a red-banded weever, a member of the tropical family to which the blue cod also belongs. It is found in northern waters to as far south as the Bay of Plenty.

Triplefins

Propped on slender pelvic fins, alertly scanning their surroundings with prominent eyes, the triplefins and blennies form a miniature society within the reef fish community. Smallness enables them to adapt to a very wide range of habitats, there being many more food niches available to small animals. They have complex social and breeding behaviours. Many have camouflage colours to blend with drab environments, or to merge with the richly variegated colours of the rock face, while others are brightly coloured, territorial fishes, with advertising coloration that enables the population to space out to best advantage.

Triplefins and blennies are a key link in the marine food chain. Eaten by a variety of predatory reef fish, they themselves browse on invertebrates too small for larger fishes. In turn, their prey feed on microscopic plants. The only living things capable of using the sun's energy to synthesise carbohydrates, plants provide the basic food of all animals.

Each species of triplefin has its special diet, from the tentacles of hydroids to shellfish eggs, barnacle cirri, tiny worms, minute shellfish, and all manner of small crustaceans. Several species remove parasitic lice from larger fishes, and nip off white fungal growths from fins and infected areas.

The triplefins found around offshore islands are generally brightly coloured, while those of tide pools and coastal waters are usually camouflaged to suit their particular habitat. As with most of the brightly coloured species, the males put on courtship colours during the spawning season, with changes in body pattern and gaily adorned fins.

Blue-eyed triplefin, see p. 118.

Banded triplefin *Forsterygion malcolmi* TL 14 cm

Immensely variable, the banded triplefin often has six irregular orange-brown bars along its body; the head is splotched apricot. Winter spawning males are near black in colour. The banded triplefin is found throughout New Zealand waters. It is also known as the mottled triplefin.

Estuarine triplefin *Grahamina nigripenne* TL 10 cm

J. Doak

The estuarine triplefin has a highly variable colour pattern: mottled, banded, splotched in green-yellow and grey-green; the gill covers are mauve. During winter, spawning males darken in tone. The species is found throughout New Zealand in estuaries, harbours, and mangrove-filled areas.

Blue-eyed triplefin *Notoclinops segmentatus* TL 6 cm

The blue-eyed triplefin has a white body with seven red bands and iridescent eye rings. It stands out boldly among the red sponges, emerald-green bryozoans and pink corals of the cliff face. During spawning, from early spring to summer, the hind-body of the male is a sooty colour, while the head becomes orange. Males guard nests in small crevices on the steep sea cliff where they are well protected but very hard to observe. The species is widespread around New Zealand, especially the north-east of the North Island, from the shallows to around 25 m.

Variable triplefin *Forsterygion varium* TL 20 cm

Variable triplefins nesting, male on left.

In late June a pair of variable triplefins are courting on the side of a sloping rock. The male wears his nuptial colours: his body a smooth satin black, the three dorsal fins made more conspicuous with a fringe of sky blue. All his three dorsal fins are held erect to magnify his size. He makes aggressive rushes at a large red moki threatening his nest site. Placated, he returns to his mottled red-fawn, green-tinged female. Both begin to quiver, side by side. The female's belly ripples like a belly dancer's, until the tip of her tail begins to quiver. The movement increases until her whole body is shaking. This seems to excite the male. He approaches, dashes away and darts back to the nest. Then he puts his pelvic fins on her, erects all other fins and begins to shudder. Such bouts of courtship may continue for two weeks or more before spawning takes place. This contrasts with the demoiselle and black angelfish, where egg laying and fertilisation immediately follow courtship. During spawning, the female's ovipositor strokes the rock, depositing a single layer of tiny eggs, which the male fertilises as they are stuck in place. His nuptial colours now fade. For a few days the couple remain together on the nest, but eventually the male remains alone, savagely repelling intruders until the eggs hatch. A male usually mates with several females and may establish as many as nine nests over the winter breeding season. Other triplefins have similar spawning patterns, but are much more secretive and difficult to observe. The variable triplefin is widespread around New Zealand, but grows larger in the south.

Common triplefin *Forsterygion lapillum* TL 8 cm

W. Farrelly

Very much a coastal species of tide pools, shallow reefs, boulders and cobbles, and often in estuaries and harbours, the common triplefin forages in the open for very small crustaceans. It varies in colour from white to greenish brown, with a distinctive black stripe from head to tail base. In their breeding season, June to January, males become dark green-black, especially on the head. They defend territories, attracting multiple females to their nest to spawn. Then they guard a patch of up to 3000 eggs for about 20 days until they hatch. They usually die after two breeding seasons. The common triplefin is widespread around New Zealand.

Yellow-black triplefin *Forsterygion flavonigrum* TL 7 cm

Yellow-black triplefin, normal coloration.

Yellow-black triplefin, male, winter courtship colours.

The yellow-black triplefin usually has a white fore-body striped with black and a yellow rear half. But at winter spawning time the male's head becomes black. The species is widespread around New Zealand coasts.

Yaldwyn's triplefin *Notoclinops yaldwyni* TL 8 cm

With Yaldwyn's triplefin, winter spawning males change from pale brown, speckled with black like the female, to a gorgeous yellow-orange; the head is pale green. The species is widespread around New Zealand coasts.

Spectacled triplefin *Ruanoho whero* TL 8 cm

The spectacled triplefin is pale orange-red, with distinctive black spectacles, but at winter spawning time the male is near black. The species is widespread around New Zealand.

Blue-dot triplefin *Notoclinops caerulepunctus* TL 5 cm

W. Farrelly

The tiny blue-dot triplefin has eight blue-black splotches along its body, bracketing luminous blue dots; it has red speckled cheeks. It spawns in spring-summer. This triplefin cleans the skin of fishes such as the toadstool grouper. The species is widespread around New Zealand.

Scaly-headed triplefin *Karalepis stewarti* TL 20 cm

The scaly-headed triplefin resembles a miniature scorpionfish, with rough, bony armour on its head; its body is mottled red, brown and white with seven wavy, red-brown bands. A nocturnal species, its camouflage makes it very hard to see, as it rests in cracks and crevices by day. At winter spawning time males are pale mauve. The species is widespread around our shores and it is restricted to New Zealand.

Oblique-swimming triplefin *Obliquichthys maryannae* TL 8 cm

Found above the crests of the kelp forest, alongside cliff walls and swarming in small rocky alcoves, the oblique-swimming triplefin is most unusual. The only triplefins known to swim in schools, oblique-swimmers are plankton-feeders. Their yellow and black bodies are constantly darting and undulating almost like a swarm of bees, as they snatch minute prey from the current. Unlike the bottom-dwelling blennies, their eyes are at the sides of the head instead of on top. The lips are not protuberant and the head is more rounded. Except when spawning in winter, they seldom rest on the rock face. During spawning males darken in tone. If alarmed, schools dart en masse into crevices or hover beneath seaweed fronds. The species is widespread around New Zealand.

Brown topknot *Notoclinus compressus* TL 13 cm

W. Farrelly

This triplefin matches the crested weedfish (next page) in almost every way: colour, shape and lifestyle. But it has three dorsal fins camouflaged with see-through 'windows'. Moving between seaweed fronds, it mimics a morsel of kelp by swimming upside down, its body rigid, sculling with rapid beats of its pectorals. While it is quite common in the shallows, this amazing strategy makes it very hard to discern. It feeds on small, weed-dwelling crustaceans. The brown topknot is widespread around New Zealand, but is more abundant in northern and central areas.

Crested weedfish *Cristiceps aurantiacus* TL 25 cm

W. Farrelly

Another master of disguise, the crested weedfish uses especially adapted pelvic and pectoral fins to walk over kelp fronds in search of prey animals that settle there, especially crustaceans; it also takes small fishes. Its body is orange-brown with variable splotches; a dark bar masks the eye. The two large dorsal fins, its shape, colour and the way it moves all conspire to render it almost invisible. Even when shifting to another kelp bush it moves over the reef like a loose scrap of weed. The crested weedfish is found in northern waters to as far south as about Hawke Bay. In Australia it is known as the golden weedfish and there it has been observed hiding among clumps of drift seaweed out on the sand. Females give birth to live young; up to 400 offspring having been recorded. This would increase the chances of the young recruiting back into the locality rather than drifting away as eggs on the currents.

Blue mimic blenny *Plagiotremus rhinorhynchos* TL 12 cm

Blue mimic blenny is a rare tropical straggler with a similar lifestyle to our common mimic blenny, but it is able to mimic either the tropical cleaner wrasse *Labroides*, when the female is dark blue with a black median stripe; or a yellow pseudanthiid, when the male is golden yellow with two thin blue stripes. In our waters it hovers alone near the sea cliff, unable to find any appropriate decoy to mimic for its surprise attacks. It is found around the Poor Knights Islands. (The example on this page was photographed at Lord Howe Island.)

Crested blenny *Parablennius laticlavius* TL 8 cm

From a vacant barnacle shell the crested blenny peers quizzically, each eye adorned with a feathery cirrus. Its body is white with a dark brown stripe; the head is blunt. Blennies make their home in disused tube worm or barnacle shells, adhering to the cliff. During winter, males entice females to deposit eggs in these shells, which the males then guard fiercely until they hatch. Crested blennies are sought after for cleaning by demoiselles that huddle in groups over the blenny nest site. The blenny darts out and cleans their gills, but it will steal the demoiselles' eggs in summer, when it is vigorously repelled. The crested blenny is found around the North Island to about Cook Strait. It is restricted to New Zealand.

Mimic blenny *Plagiotremus tapeinosoma* TL 10 cm

The observant diver may notice something odd among a swarm of oblique-swimmers: a stranger in their midst. It is the mimic blenny. In tropical seas, similar blennies imitate the swimming movements, fin patterns and markings of the cleaner wrasse. By this subterfuge the mimic is able to approach fishes that are anxious to be cleaned. It dances up in the fashion of the true cleaner, but instead uses the fish's trust to make a vicious attack, nipping off a small portion of the host's fins or skin. Similarly, this species mimics the harmless little oblique-swimming triplefin to its own advantage. Once in clear focus, the mimic gives itself away by its longer body and more sinuous swimming movements. While it seeks acceptance in the school, it is not fully in tune with its models. Its predatory mouth is not at the front of its head, but, like a shark's, is concealed on the underside, and, unlike its plankton-feeding model, the mimic has needle-sharp teeth. By swimming with these harmless triplefins, the mimic blenny is able to get close to larger fishes. A lightning attack on the unsuspecting victim's fins puts it to flight with startled rapidity. In nature, mimicry achieves a variety of purposes. Butterflies mimic wasps to gain protection; orchids mimic wasps for pollination; and a harmless snake eel imitates a poisonous sea snake so perfectly that only an expert can tell the difference. At spawning time male mimic blennies retreat into a disused tube worm shell or barnacle, wriggling in backwards until just the head is visible. They court females and induce them to lay their eggs in the nest, guarding them until they hatch. The mimic blenny can be found around northern New Zealand to as far south as the Bay of Plenty.

J Doak

Possibly because of climate change, three Australian gobies have recently settled in our northern harbours, estuaries and mangrove rivers. One is called the exquisite sand goby. Gobies are the largest family of marine fishes with some 1500 species worldwide, mostly tropical. This sand goby is distinguished from triplefins by having just two dorsal fins on which it has orange-red spots that continue on to the rounded tail. In summer it has been seen entering an inverted cockleshell valve for refuge or possibly to nest. It does not use a burrow as does a fellow migrant, the bridled goby, *Arenigobius bifrenatus*. It appears to inflate its abdomen as a threat gesture. Aggregations of around 20 are seen.

127

PLEURONECTIDAE

W. Farrelly

It is hard to believe that the sand flounder, like all its relatives, begins life as a normal, upright fish. As it develops from the larval stage, one eye migrates to the upper side of the body, leaving the underside blind. So, in fact the adult swims on its side, with the continuous dorsal fin fringing one edge of its distinctive diamond-shaped body and the extended anal fin on the other. It skims the bottom with undulating ripples running along its body and fins, scanning ahead for prey with its protruding eyes. The sand flounder is excellently adapted for night feeding (sometimes by day) on invertebrates in sand or mud, such as crabs, shrimps, worms, shellfish and even tiny fishes. For defence, its skin has special pigment cells that enable it to match the colour of its surroundings rapidly. It needs no swim bladder and only leaves the bottom during courtship and spawning activities. Early years are spent in harbours and estuaries. The fish matures at about 25 cm. Sand flounder leave sheltered waters in spring (winter in the north) to spawn inshore. They live about eight years. The species is restricted to New Zealand and is widespread.

Leatherjacket *Parika scaber* TL 40 cm

Leatherjacket, females.

The leatherjacket grazes sponge tissue with great gusto, a diet few fishes would accept because it is full of needle-sharp spicules and toxic slime. With their chisel-like teeth and very powerful jaws leatherjackets will even attack a sea urchin, gradually nipping the spines away to smash the shell and gorge its contents. Their catholic taste may be the secret of their success – they are found everywhere around New Zealand, from the shallows to 100 m. It has been calculated that, where abundant, these bottom-biters modify 20 per cent of the rock face every year, helping to maintain the patchwork-quilt diversity of life forms. The leatherjacket has few predators. As well as its rigid body and tough skin, it has a large serrated dorsal spine for defence. Along its hind margin is a deep, V-shaped groove into which fits another wedge-shaped spine. When the first spine is erected, the second, the so-called 'trigger', locks it firmly into position. Unless muscles retract the trigger, the main spine cannot be depressed. Any predator that swallowed such a meal would damage its intestines. When alarmed, or even when on the defensive, as when feeding or putting on a sexual or aggressive display, the dorsal spine is raised like a flag. The leatherjacket has no pelvic fins. Backward-angled, soft dorsal and anal fins ripple with waves, driving it forward or, when required, in reverse. The tail forms a stabilising vane. Gill openings, vulnerable areas in most fishes, are reduced to tiny slits. The body is encased in a thick, inflexible hide, the normal scales having been modified into bony spinules, like coarse sandpaper. At night leatherjackets shelter in crevices, their skin mottled with white, dorsal spines erect. During winter males establish territories repelling other males and attracting a female with an elaborate display of sexual colours. The head develops light blue markings with dark, oblique stripes radiating from the eye. The dorsal spine is waggled up and down suggestively and the widespread, lemon yellow tail is waved vertically. The female's body is a mosaic of dark mottling. Courtship is intensive, with weeks of frantic pursuits. Paired spawning has been observed in August when nests of unguarded eggs are made. Juveniles appear in summer, minute green replicas about 50 mm long, sheltering amid the kelp. Growth is rapid and they attain adult size in two years. The leatherjacket is also known as triggerfish.

Leatherjacket, male, in courtship display.

129

Sharp-nosed pufferfish *Canthigaster callisterna* TL 20 cm

Another versatile bottom grazer, the sharp-nosed pufferfish is most prevalent where there are many caves and rocky galleries. Up to 50 may inhabit one labyrinth. In other areas they hover 5 m above the sand. Individuals stalk shrimps around bushes of sargassum weed. When disturbed, the puffer inflates its swim bladder with water, increasing its size. The variable white stripe on its side is a warning: parts of its body are deadly poisonous. Like its relatives the porcupinefish and sunfish, the puffer has teeth fused into a beak, divided in front. This suits it to a very broad diet, with sponge a speciality. The gills are just tiny slits, as its rigid skeleton would restrict the pump action of bony gill covers. To compensate, the fish has a rapid respiratory cycle of up to 150 movements per minute. It has no spiny dorsal fin at all, and only the skimpiest of tails, which it uses for displays of courtship and aggression. Propulsion is by means of opposed dorsal and anal fins. The rear part of its body is so shaped that these fins give adequate forward thrust. The sharp-nosed pufferfish is found around northern New Zealand to as far south as the Bay of Plenty. The species is also known as the clown toado.

The flesh of the porcupinefish is extremely poisonous. Its powerful jaws can crush invertebrates: large molluscs, urchins and crustaceans that most fishes cannot eat. Large porcupinefishes are home ranging. They are usually found in moderate depths, down to 20 m, swimming among kelp forests and never far from rocky underhangs and ledges. The porcupinefish has a highly developed swim bladder. When provoked, the fish distends itself enormously by drawing in water through its mouth. It takes more than a minute to inflate its swim bladder fully. As the body distends, the sharp, three-pointed spines embedded in the skin, although permanently erect, become even more forbidding. With its rigid body armour the porcupinefish has a peculiar swimming style. Propulsion comes from the rear-facing opposing dorsal and anal fins, while the tail is just a small steering vane. Because of its peculiar body shape the pectoral fins, used for pitching movements, are unusually high up on the sides, level with the eyes, compared with other fishes. In southern waters a more common relative is the globefish, *Contusus richei*, a much smaller fish, with a total length of 13 cm, and with less prominent spines that only become erect when it inflates. The porcupinefish is widespread around the coasts and is restricted to New Zealand.

Sunfish *Mola mola* TL 300 cm

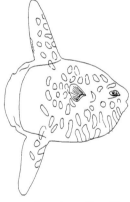

A pelagic relative of the leather-jacket, puffer and porcupine-fish, the sunfish is the most bizarre of all: a head with two fins and a tail flap. Its spinal cord is no more than 25 mm long, this for a fish weighing over a ton. Its body forms an oval disc with two long opposed fins placed towards one end, bridged by a hinged crescent-shaped flap serving as a tail. This huge fish is served by a tiny mouth with a bony-ridged jaw. It feeds on soft-bodied plankton: salps and jellyfishes, but the strong jaw appears adapted to crushing shellfishes and crustaceans from the seafloor. The propulsive system is most unusual. The two long fins move in unison from side to side, each describing a figure of eight, counteracted by the large tail surface. With the inertia of such a huge animal it takes some time for this type of finning to accelerate, but it can leap right out of the sea. Sunfish appear in northern waters from November to late June. The most common period for sightings is December to January, when large numbers are seen, dorsal fins waving above the surface. Stragglers reach as far south as the Otago Peninsula.

Glossary

Abdomen belly.

Amphipod small, laterally compressed crustacean.

Anal fin between anus and tail.

Ascidian sea squirt or tunicate.

Barbel sensory tentacle beneath chin.

Bryozoa tiny colonial creatures resembling corals or sea plants.

Canine long, conical tooth.

Cartilaginous having skeleton of gristle.

Caudal the tail region.

Caudal peduncle links fish body to tail.

Chemoreception senses of taste and smell.

Chiton limpet-like gastropod.

Ciliated having mobile, hair-like processes.

Cirri tentacles; may branch.

Cnidaria marine relatives of the hydras or polyps: anemones, corals, gorgonians etc.

Copepod small, planktonic crustacean.

Countershading dark dorsum; pale below.

Crustacean hard-shelled arthropods like crabs, shrimps.

Cryptic camouflage resembles background.

Cusp point.

Dermal the back.

Disruptive camouflage irregular contrasting patches.

Diurnal active by day.

Dominance hierarchy pecking order.

Dorsal fin on the fish's back.

Dorsum the back.

Echinoid of sea urchin group.

Euphausiid shrimp pelagic crustacean; krill.

Filamentous long, thin.

Gill filament slender structure that absorbs oxygen.

Gill plate protective cover of respiratory organ.

Ground colour overall basic colour.

Guild group of fish with similar lifestyle.

Gyre rotating current.

Hermaphroditic bisexual.

Home ranging living within a defined area.

Hydroid polyp-style cnidarian.

Invertebrates animals without backbones.

Isopod small, flattened crustacean. Sea louse.

Larva first stage of development from egg.

Larval fish translucent, pelagic juvenile.

Lateral compression flattened from side to side.

Lateral line sensory organ along fish's side.

Lunate crescent-shaped.

Median along the middle.

Median fins dorsal, anal and caudal.

Mysid tiny, shrimp-like crustacean.

Nape on head, behind eyes.

Nocturnal active by night.

Obliterative effect rendering hard to see.

Ocellus eye-like spot.

Oesophagus food tube between mouth and stomach.

Olfactory organ smell sensor.

Opposed opposite sides.

Ovipositor tube through which eggs are extruded.

Paired fins pectoral and ventral fins.

Pectoral fins those on sides behind gill slits.

Peduncle area between body and tail.

Pelagic of the open ocean.

Pelvic fins lower fins behind gills.

Pharyngeal teeth grinding mill in throat.

Plankton tiny plants and animals of the open ocean.

Polymorphic passing through several forms.

Protrusile jaws expandable jaws.

Radiation process whereby species evolve to fit new niches.

Salp gelatinous pelagic tunicate (marine animal with rubbery outer coat).

Scutes thin bony plates.

Sex reversal gender switching.

Sexual dimorphism distinct gender forms.

Speciation formation of species by evolution.

Spicule rod-like spine.

Spinule small spine.

Subtropics the warm region between the tropics and the cooler temperate region.

Tactile having sense of touch.

Tail lobe protruding part of tail fin.

Teleost bony fish.

Territorial defending a home range.

Transverse waves running along the long axis.

Tricuspid teeth having three cusps or points.

Variegated varied in colour.

Ventral fins lower fins near anus.

Zooplankton tiny animals living in open waters.

Further reading

Ayling, T. and Cox, C.J. 1982. *Collins Guide to the Sea Fishes of New Zealand*. Collins, Auckland.

Doak, W.T. 1978. *Fishes of the New Zealand Region*. Second edition. Hodder and Stoughton, Auckland.

Doak, W.T. 1980. *The Cliff Dwellers*. Hodder and Stoughton, Auckland.*

Doak, W.T. 1991. *Wade Doak's World of New Zealand Fishes*. Hodder and Stoughton, Auckland.*

Edney, G. 2001. *Poor Knights Wonderland*. Sea Tech Ltd, Auckland.

Francis, M. 2001. *Coastal Fishes of New Zealand*. Third edition. Reed Publishing, Auckland.

Graham, D.H. 1956. *A Treasury of New Zealand Fishes*. Second edition. Reed, Wellington.

Paul, L. 2000. *New Zealand Fishes. Identification, natural history and fisheries*. Revised edition. Reed Publishing, Auckland.

Paulin, C. and Roberts, C. 1992. *The Rockpool Fishes of New Zealand*. Museum of New Zealand, Te Papa Tongarewa, Wellington.

Paulin, C., Stewart, A., Roberts, C. and McMillan, P. 1989. *New Zealand Fish: A Complete Guide*. National Museum of New Zealand Miscellaneous Series 19.

* Available per www.wadedoak.com

Index of common names

Index of scientific names

Notes

Notes